Ranger School, May-September, 1989

I started out with 48 other Infantry 2nd Lieutenants in a class
of 600. Most of the other ~550 were folks that had already

gone through some kind of "pre-Ranger" training so they were a leg up on us Infantry 2Lt's. After a week there were only seven of the 48 left. At the end, there were only two. Of the 600 hard chargers, about 80% wouldn't make it.

Six guys that summer had to be resuscitated with a defibrillator. They had wanted to make it so badly that they had kept pushing no matter the danger signals from their body.

There were hard times. I cried like a school girl when Warren Eby walked up to a Ranger Instructor and said "I quit." In the first week we put 150 of the class in the hospital for heat exhaustion. I failed a leadership position in the final phase and will never forget the horror of being removed from my class as they proceeded to graduate, nor the fury at the unfairness of the decision.

There were good times. The finest thing a person has ever done for me was to give me half of his field ration cookie bar when I was at the end of my emergency reserves, lying pitifully in 12" of cold water, shivering, and with legs so cramped up they wouldn't work.

Ranger School helps you figure out how to function and lead when you and your people are under very difficult conditions. The group plans and executes small unit missions, while subject to extremes of physical exhaustion made more difficult by significant chow and sleep deprivation. The candidates have to find undiscovered reserves of tenacity to keep functioning. They have to find ways to help and encourage the candidates around them to function despite the hardships, and they have to stay healthy. Most of the candidates aren't able to overcome these obstacles and therefore there's a very high attrition rate. The survivors learned a great deal about themselves, and about leading others under difficult conditions. Thousands of times I told myself, "you are not dead yet. Keep going." Ranger School builds confidence

It takes much more energy to lead then to follow. When each person is physically exhausted and being punished by day after day of cold, wet, or heat, it is the leader's example of endurance and tenacity that they draw strength from. Providing that example sucks the life out of the leader, who is under constant, unrelenting observation day and night. There is never a moment's respite from the responsibility to provide the inexhaustible enthusiastic example that buoys the morale of the organization.

.

Everyone had their own strengths and weaknesses. What was especially difficult for one person was often less so for another.

Sleep deprivation. At its worst we went five days and nights of moving, planning and patrolling on a total of 20 minutes of rack time. That is to say, on the fifth night, we got 20 minutes of shut-eye. Lack of sleep didn't impact me as hard as it did some others. I seemed to be able to continue to function at a base level pretty much infinitely on no sleep, as long as I could keep moving and no one expected me to think. If I stopped moving, staying awake was quite difficult.

I spent a great deal of time at Ranger trying to stay awake. Whenever I stopped moving, I had to very carefully watch where my mind wandered because it seemed impossible to spot the seamless transition to sleep. Given the consequences of falling asleep, it was really quite worrisome how I could be "sure" that I was wide awake, yet be sound asleep.

Watching where your mind wanders. It is hard to describe how one might monitor their own thoughts. I had to discipline myself to, whenever I wasn't moving, to constantly ask myself if I was still in some awful nightmare of starvation and exhaustion. When I occasionally found myself rested and eating, no matter how real it seemed, I had to be dreaming. It took an emergency dose of will and adrenalin to raise a desperate, shrieking alarm that would jolt my addled brain back to wakefulness.

In the absence of sleep, if someone told me something, I had to painstakingly write it down because I couldn't seem to remember very well. When I took notes I'd form each written character with painstaking care, because I knew that I was going to need those critical notes. Often later, to my horror, I'd find only indecipherable chicken scratches. It was really quite irritating to vividly recall how careful I was to take perfect notes yesterday, yet see only chicken scratches today.

Sleep deprivation also impacted long term memory. Most of my recollections of Ranger School are from the first week. After that it gets fuzzy

Chow deprivation. The lack of chow was hard on me, much harder than the sleep deprivation. Every week or so we received a week's worth of chow, 7 MRE field rations, to stuff into our rucks. We probably burned 3 times that. Because I started running in HS and then did a long tour in college, I'd been a runner, cyclist, and ultimately a triathlete, for 13yrs before I started Ranger School. I would not have thought that I had more than a couple pounds I could lose, but over the course of the 3 months, I lost 25lbs. The body is quick to consume muscle mass if it's is starving because muscles burn calories. Less muscle means a body that can survive with less food. Take 25lbs from a 6' tall runner and you end up with a scarecrow.

At the start of Ranger I could do 120 pushups. Coming out I'd do 10 and collapse. My body was a wreck. I'd have done virtually anything--paid any price for food during Ranger School. I spent hours every day fantasizing about food. I resolved that after Ranger I would, every waking hour for the rest of my life, have a packet of Pop-Tarts in my pocket. Cinnamon Pop-Tarts. Best with chocolate frosting on top.

Although it was the right season for berries, the odd bush we'd find was usually picked clean. As kids in OR/WA we'd routinely snacked on berries in the woods, but the berries native to GA/FL weren't the same. I was really hungry, but poisoning myself would have made things a lot worse, I figured. I imagined a scenario where my unhappy digestive system started emptying out though both ends during hours of constant movement. That would be really quite bad, I thought. I considered worms and bugs, but dirty and raw made them seem very unappealing. I was getting thin, but I wasn't dying.

The challenge, moment by moment, was to not let the hardships prevent you from giving 110% to your squad at all times. An illustrative example from the Desert Phase:

I'd never been so completely worn out. It wasn't the exhaustion of competition, even a triathlon. It was the exhaustion of weeks of 23-24hour days, of 8-10hrs/day moving thru vegetation and up hills carrying over 100lbs, going thru a couple gallons of water each day, and getting only about 1/3rd of calories needed. I'd been in endurance sports for over a decade. I'd been in challenging military environments for almost as long. I had been cockily sure that I could withstand physical challenges better than most. But I was near collapse. Not just tired. I'd burned thru what I'd thought to be near infinite reserves of tenacity. I had nothing left but a threadbare mantra I'd repeat, "I'm not dead yet, keep moving."

I was so worn out that each time we "took a knee," in a hasty halt, I worried that with 130lbs of ruck, weapon, and equipment, I'd not be able to get back to my feet. To get up I'd have to plant the butt of my weapon on the ground so I could use my arms to help get me up on both feet. After a supreme shove, I'd stagger drunkenly to my feet and pause while I caught my breath and my legs shook.

It was time to change responsibilities in the squad and the machine gun should go to the small guy "over there." I didn't know him very well, but he seemed to try hard. Although he was small, he carried the same load I did. Therefore he had to be in worse shape. "The heavy and cumbersome machine gun was going to be a helova lot harder on him, than me," I thought. I could see the despair in his eyes.

I went over to him and said "I want to be machine gunner today. Here, take my M16." I gave him my 7lb M16 rifle and took the M60 machinegun, 30lbs loaded, and the additional 15-20lbs of ammo.

He was too tired to say "thanks," but the relief and gratitude was plainly visible on his face.

I had done something nice. An inner smile would provide some untapped reserves that would help me for a couple hours. Carrying the thing all day was going to be a bear though.

Failing Ranger School.
There were lots of ways to fail Ranger. If you simply gave up, you were gone. If you lost 24hrs training due to a medical issue, you Recycled. That is to say, you did not move on to the next phase with your mates. Recycling meant that you were held in limbo for a couple weeks or a month until the next class came through. Then you would join a new squad and platoon.

In each of the 4 phases you had to get a "Pass" in a Leadership positions like platoon leader and squad leader. The positions were generally rotated twice per day. One leadership team would plan the mission and another would execute it. If you failed a leadership position, at the end of the phase you recycled. Or, if you were very lucky, you might get a second leadership position in that same phase and get a second chance to pass.

The prospect of recycling in FL and therefore having to do the swamp phase twice, would make a strong man weep.

The rotating leadership positions helped make us very

cooperative. Each leader was desperate to "Pass." If you were in a leadership position, I would bust my ass to help you succeed because the roles might be reversed tomorrow and I'd be desperate to get a Pass in the temporary leadership position.

After each phase we held Peer Evaluations. The guy with the lowest anonymous evaluation from his peers got Recycled. This too, encouraged us to be extremely cooperative. We didn't just try hard to get along well, we were obsessively supportive of each other. Anything one person could do to help another, we did. And this in an environment where we were all so exhausted we were half dead. If you saw someone having a tougher time than you, be it carrying a load, or an intricacy of the planning process, you helped, no matter what the cost to you.

Everyone knew who it was that made extra efforts to help others, and who didn't. The latter didn't last long. This obsession with helping your buddy permeates the entire culture of Army Rangers.

At the beginning of each phase we always got new guys, Recycles from the last class. Each squad of 10-16 would get 1-2 new guys. Those new guys were under significant pressure to perform and contribute. Some came to us as Medical Fails, but most had been Peered out of their original squad and this was their "second chance."

The rule was one couldn't get recycled for the same reason twice. So if a Recycle joined our squad because they'd been Peered out, they'd come to our family as some outsider desperate to not be Peered out a second time. They needed to be so fabulous, such strong contributors, that the squad would evaluate them higher than one of our own family. It was a high bar. Likewise, a Leadership recycle or a Medical recycle would join the next class coming through and be desperate to avoid a second Leadership or second Medical failure.

The different phases of Ranger School.
Ranger School consisted of City Week and then four phases
in the field. Darby Phase at Ft. Benning, Georgia, the
Mountain Phase in N. Georgia, the Swamp Phase at Elgin AF
Base, Florida, and the Desert Phase, then in Utah. If you
made it all the way through, it was nine weeks. I completed
the 15 week plan, having, sadly, recycled in the desert.

As all 600 of us stood in formation on the first morning and
received our introductory briefing, we were told that "although
a lot of you won't make it through City Week, you will later
remember it fondly as "the easy part of Ranger School." We
responded, of course, by rolling our eyes like teenagers.

City Week was mostly a lot of exercise. The combination of
exercise and the heat/humidity of the GA summer did in about
a third of the ~600 class. Consider that for a moment. These
were really fit and determined guys that had been training for
Ranger School for months or years. City Week was only, well,
a week. The average person would imagine that they could
put up with just about any physical regimen for a week. But
that week of exercise in the heat and humidity was rough
enough that we lost almost 200 really fit hard-chargers.

My only trial was involved getting in trouble over something
dumb and getting yelled at a bit, but some successes in Land
Navigation allowed me to avoid the threatened Recycle.

The general scheme for all of the Ranger School 2 week
phases in the field was ~12hrs of mission planning, followed
by ~12hrs of mission execution. The only breaks we got were
associated with getting us moved from one phase to another
in buses, or in the case of the move to/from Utah, C141 cargo
planes. We were, of course, jammed into these conveyances
like sardines, but being off our feet for a while and catching up
on some sleep provided for desperately needed recovery time.

Darby Phase was 2 weeks of squad patrols at Ft. Benning,

GA. The squad was really large when we started Darby, maybe 20 guys. We got a couple Recycles into the squad, guys that had failed Darby Phase in the previous class, but we also lost folks due to injury or guys simply choosing to call it quits. Although we got an honest several hours of sleep/night during City Week, during Darby Phase we only got about 30 minutes sleep per day. During City Week we'd gotten 2 big meals/day....essentially as much food as you could put away in 5min or so. In contrast, Darby Phase was the beginning of the chow deprivation that would characterize the rest of Ranger School. With the exception of one especially meager chicken dinner, we received one MRE (Meal, Ready to Eat. Colloquially understood as three lies in one) field ration per day. To add to the joy of Darby Phase, it rained every day.

Our night moves were conducted just as fast as possible. During Darby Phase we were still strong so we'd move at a near jog, carrying roughly 130lbs of ruck, weapon, etc. thru heavy vegetation and inky darkness. The requirement to move so darn fast, when we couldn't see a thing under the forest canopy, beat us up a lot. You absolutely could not see your hand in front of your face. Through inky darkness you had to walk as fast as you could, while banging shins and knees. Because of the uneven terrain and our awkward and heavy load, we routinely stumbled, sometimes catching ourselves, sometimes not. I was constantly worried that I'd fall and break a leg or blow out an ankle. To shield my eyes from unseen hazards, I kept my hat visor pulled down as best I could. I took a lot of sticks in the visor and face, but I managed to avoid losing an eye.

All one could see of the guy in front of them was two small glow-in-the-dark patches, cat-eyes we called them, sewn on to the back of his hat. Each of us concentrated on the two dancing cat-eyes on the hat in front of us. The motion of those glow-in-the-dark cat-eyes were clues as to the invisible hazards that each of us were about to stride into. Sometimes those cat-eyes disappeared down and away. Followed by the sound of your buddy tumbling down the ravine he'd just found.

The mental image of one of us very heavily laden guys stepping off, in the inky darkness, right into open air and then tumbling ass-over-teakettle into a ravine, was absolutely hysterical. But the hilarity warred with our worry re. the guy getting hurt. As a result, each time someone went crashing away from group, or the word came back "Jones fell into another ravine" the patrol would pause as we all imagined the surprise on Jones' face as his forward foot came down on nothing. Because it was so dark, it was safe enough to grin fiercely. We were all young and someone getting seriously hurt was rare. We just couldn't whisper anything to each other for fear we'd burst out laughing.

Once we heard the pissed off whisper from forward and down below…some variation of "fuck! <pause> I'm ok. Fucking help me back fucking up there." We'd stand there in line, in the heavy vegetation, none of us having moved an inch in the inky darkness, and everyone would kind of "vibrate" as we each silently howled with laughter. We'd lean against each other's rucksacks, we'd struggle to breathe, and tears would stream out of our eyes. We tried very hard not to make any audible sound of the laughter in order to protect the current leadership holders from being "light and noise discipline" failures.

Dummy cords. Because we were so tired, in such a hurry and it was so darn dark, we had to have everything tied to us or it would turn up lost in the morning. Rifles, canteens, our hats, gloves, pocket knives, notebooks, everything. My hat was tied to a my blouse's top button hole so each time a stick in the darkness snagged my hat off of my head, it would just dangle over my shoulder. I'd reach back, pop it back on my head, and pull the bill down low again. so it would keep protecting my eyes. Without it being tied to us with a dummy cord, we'd have lost our asses.

I think our squad of ~20 lost four in Darby Phase so that would have brought the squad down to 16. Even though our squad got one or two Recycles at the beginning of each phase, we always lost guys faster than we gained them. One guy got hurt falling into a ravine, another quit, and two guys got "Peered Out", a painful activity that is described in more detail elsewhere. I didn't really perceive Darby Phase as all that hard though. Sure, we operated on about 30 minutes sleep per day, and we didn't get much chow, and we were wet for two weeks, but this was just the initial weeks of Ranger School. We were still physically and mentally strong and therefore capable of enduring the 24hr cycle of planning and executing patrols without digging deep into our reserves of strength and tenacity.

Mountain phase, in North Georgia near the town of Dahlonega, was difficult. With rucksacks, weapons and equipment often over 130lbs, we climbed up endless ridges, often so steep that we were down on all fours clawing our way up. We became so exhausted, trying to carry our combat load up the hills, that we were reduced to six inch baby steps.

I don't recall that we ever got dry in the mountains, so by the end of the phase we'd been wet for four weeks. Even though it was summer, it got chilly in the higher elevations so whenever we stopped moving, my teeth started chattering. When you are motionless, wet, and cold, a night can seem to take a week to slowly creep by.

It was wet and overcast thru the entire mountain phase except for one afternoon when the sun came out and warmed our faces thru the canopy of trees up above. The sun cheered us up very much that day.

During Mountain Phase we also did some rappelling and some knot tying. The only difficult rappel was the buddy-rappel that simulated bringing a casualty down a cliff. I volunteered to be the one that took the weight of the biggest guy in the squad. Someone had to do it and I was less exhausted than most. It was a near thing though. Upper-body strength wasn't my forte' and supporting the 130lbs of rucksack, gear and my weapon, and the casualty's 200 additional pounds, took everything I had. I made my way carefully down the cliff, making short moves that I could control, and making darn sure of my grip each time I came to a halt. I did what I could to carry a little of the weight on my legs. In the last half of the drop, I was losing strength so rapidly that I was terrified that I'd drop the guy. I barely made it down to the bottom. Then I toppled over and lay on the ground for a while, my muscles shaking from the effort.

It frightened me that I'd almost run out of strength, which would have resulted in dropping the guy on to the rocks far below. But I was pretty sure that I had the most strength remaining of the squad. By normal standards we were all quite fit, but Hollywood depicts elite military types as weightlifter and gymnast body-types and that's not real. The most significant individual attribute of elite forces is not the mass of their muscles, but their tenacity and self-discipline. Me volunteering to take the biggest guy down almost had terrible consequences, but someone was going to have to take him so what was the better choice?

The knot tying examination was less successful. I practiced quite a bit for the knot tying test and, of course, failed it. Hearing the explanation for my failure was like trying to follow what a Yankee is saying at an inflectionless 1000 words/minute because they've been telling people the same spiel for the last year. The Ranger Instructor said something completely incomprehensible like "fail for asymmetrical locking bar" and that was that. I worried about the about consequences of failing the knot tying test, so I kept my ears open for a knot tying test redo, or maybe an opportunity to work off a demerit or something. Knot tying was never brought up again. No consequences, no test re-do, nothing.

Uncharacteristically, I kept my mouth shut and did not inquire as the consequence of the knot tying failure.

Our squad gained a Recycle at the start of Mountain Phase, but three called it quits because carrying all that weight up those mountains did them in. The lack of food, sleep, and recovery time, made us weaker and weaker with each passing day. On a number of occasions, I carried some gear for other guys, especially smaller guys. I wasn't dancing up those hills either, but I seemed to find a steady-state that was sustainable. Try as we might, we couldn't keep our feet dry so a lot of us were getting holes in our feet. We also lost a guy to Peering out, so four total.

That's how hard Mountain was. The squad had been though a lot before we got to the Mountains. City Week removed the weak. Darby Phase removed those that were insufficiently motivated. So the candidates that made it to the Mountains were a pretty tough and hard charging bunch, but we still lost a quarter of our squad.

It was a long bus ride from North Georgia to the Florida Panhandle. We were packed like sardines into busses. We took off our boots and socks so that they and our feet might dry out. Then we slumped in sleep for the day-long bus ride.

When we got to Eglin AF Base, the home of the Florida swamp phase, we had a helova time getting our boots on. Everyone was sure that they'd mixed up their boots with the guy next to them. There was chaos as 30 some-odd guys, all with huge rucksacks in their laps and the aisles stacked with dufflebags, all tried to swap boots with each other. It took us a while to figure out that, incredibly, our feet had swollen a couple full shoe-sizes.

After pulling ourselves to our feet, we found that we could only barely walk. Our legs, exhausted from 5wks of toil, then having spent ~10hrs bent and motionless in the crowded bus, wouldn't support us.

Our attempt to get into a formation outside of the bus was a hapless comedy of highly motivated, anxious to please, fit adult males trying to move as directed without the embarrassment of crawling. Interrupted while we were trying to sort out the boot confusion, some of us had one boot on, while others were carrying boots they'd found in their vicinity, having rejected their own boots as "can't be mine—too small." Our gear, tossed out the bus's rear fire-door, was piled in a chaotic unmilitary mess that drew ire immediately.

We could not stand. We sat there on our scattered gear for a bit. We were dazed by being pulled out of our first sound sleep in weeks. The Ranger Instructors berated us. We rubbed our legs, moved our joints, and tried to get up. We were pitiful wretches, but we couldn't help but be amused at madness of the scene. Only the hollering of the instructors prevented us from bursting out with laughter at our own helplessness.

Whereas the Mountain Phase primarily required fitness, the Swamp Phase required so much more. We'd been worked to exhaustion every day for 5wks. For most of that, we'd received darn little chow and sleep. We, the survivors of the Mountain Phase, were desperate for a couple days to let our legs recover from struggling our 130lbs of gear up those hills day and night. Our weakened state made us easy prey for illnesses, so most everyone was fighting some kind of bug. Our feet, knees, and various chafe-points, were open sores. The swamps and rain ensured that we remained wet for two more weeks. We counted coup that we were outlasting our equipment. Our nylon Cordura rucksacks were fraying and their metal frames were breaking.

Folks were so worn out by the time they got to the Swamp Phase that there were a lot of Medical Recycles. We'd been wet for so many days that skin rotting off was a common malady. Our Squad got two or three Recycles, but we probably lost three by the end of the phase....all of them just called it quits. Every guy we lost in Florida was a guy that had made it through very difficult times in the weeks previous. But we were in bad shape and Florida was tough. Only the most tenacious made it thru the Swamp Phase.

The Desert Phase, in the high desert of Utah, was kind of fun.

We got gloriously dry, and we participated in live-fire exercises more realistic than any I'd ever been involved in. As a safety precaution for the live-fires, we were granted a couple hours honest sleep/night. We lost relatively few Ranger Candidates during the final Desert Phase, but to my endless aggravation, I was one. I was a Desert Phase Recycle.

Attrition. We started with ~600. Over the course of the 5 training environments, we received ~100 Recycles from the previous Ranger Class, so call it ~700 folks, the vast majority of whom were highly motivated and well prepared. We ultimately graduated ~150 for an attrition rate of ~79%. Of us 48 Infantry 2Lt's, two of us made it.

The saga of Warren Eby.
Eby and I were tight. We had been thru Officer Candidate School (OCS) together and then Infantry Officer Basic. He was a quiet and serious guy so I didn't get to know him very well until he started participating in some hijinks with me and the hilarious Officer Candidate Green during the last month of OCS.

Towards the end of OCS Green and I were a bit out of control at night during field exercises. We'd try to figure out how to cause as much trouble as possible for the "Opposing Forces" (OPFOR) squad that would inevitably try to attack the OCS Company's defensive position. In the pursuit of this fun, we would happily discard all common sense.

For example, we would try to figure out where, out in the woods that surrounded our perimeter, the OPFOR (Opposing Forces) types were likely to collect before moving towards our position to launch their attack. A dirt road, that came within a mile of our front lines a couple ridgelines away, would be an obvious location for them to be dropped off by truck. This drop off/pick up site would, from their perspective, be an administrative area. Besides, the scripted affair had them moving through the woods a bit to shoot up a bunch of hapless officer candidates, then withdraw back to their trucks so they could go home and get warm.

Bernie was very "off-script". If we could figure out where their drop-off site was, we could attack them when they were in admin mode, always in darkness, while they offloaded, or loaded back up.

Often, Green and I, and later Eby would volunteer to be a permanent Listening Post forward of friendly lines. That gave us relative freedom to cause whatever chaos we, usually Green, dreamed up. We just had to take care that we couldn't be identified.

2LT Warren Eby, One of the most terrific guys I've ever had the luck to be near. We're no longer in touch, which is sad as hell. I will always miss him. Picture taken at a not particularly useful Infantry Officer Basic Course field exercise, Ft. Benning, GA, Spring 1989.

The OCS Company position often got attacked at night. We'd abandon our Listening Post and charge into the attackers as they traded shots with our classmates. From a tactical standpoint, it was mostly insane. But we'd lost our minds and treated it all like paintball, racing thru the enemy, shooting everyone we saw and delivering the odd body-slam or foot stomp as we charged by. With the anonymity provided by the darkness, we were kind of hard on folks. Then we'd race back to our Listening Post, howling with laughter. The real challenge, once the attack was over and the sorry OCS Cadre Officers shrieked for a formation to figure out what the fuck just happened, was to try not to giggle. In the darkness, no one can see you grin.

I'd love to take credit for those adventures, but it was really all Green's doing. I'm risk averse by nature, but Green would pull any stunt for a laugh and to the devil with consequences. He was one of the most hilarious guys I've ever known.

Twice, after an attack, we managed to follow the OPFOR back to their laager site, wait until they sacked out, then assault them with artillery simulators, blank machine gun fire, and trample them in their sleeping bags. Our best effort ever was when we followed the OPFOR back to their site, and found that they were getting into trucks. It was totally dark. No one could see anyone's faces. So we got into the trucks with them. But as soon as the trucks started moving, we leaped up and machine gunned everyone with M16's on full auto. Then we jumped out of the back of the slowly moving trucks and ran into the woods howling with laughter.

In retrospect, we're lucky we didn't seriously hurt anyone. We were young, dumb, indestructible, and somehow stupidly sure we'd never get in any serious trouble. The hijinks were absolutely hilarious. Merging with the OPFOR, spending several minutes trying to act as one of their group in the darkness, participating in mono-syllable conversations, grunting out a name to appease a SGT taking roll, as I climbed into the back of the big truck that was to take them all home, all the time elbowing Green and stifling giggles, was an unforgettable night of hilarity.

After spending the first half of OCS being quiet and earnest, Eby finally came out of his shell and started hanging out with Green and I when we were in the field. He then participated in our madcap anti-OPFOR operations with great gusto. He was a very stoic guy so not given to casual expressions of emotion. We'd charge thru the OPFOR attack from their flank, taking them completely by surprise, Eby firing hundreds of rounds of blanks from his M60 machine gun and me lighting artillery simulators that Green had swiped, once again, from the cadre. Eby was somehow able to drape, what seemed to be 20 feet of machine gun ammo belt over himself and keep it all under control as he raced thru the woods blasting away with the M60. Like Rambo, he fired the M60 with one hand as he controlled the ammo belt with the other. I'm pretty sure that when we snuck back to our own fighting positions, that I saw Eby crack a smile. Warren Eby was not one to wantonly display unnecessary emotions. It had to be important.

After Officer Candidate School, Eby and I went to Infantry Officer Basic together. We were in the same platoon of a couple dozen. The cadre officer in charge of us, a sorry example of an Infantry Captain, put Eby and I in charge of the platoon. He and I were coming from OCS, were both prior service, and were trying to act the part of (oxymoron alert) mature young officers. In contrast, the other kids were all from ROTC or West Point. The ROTC kids were all pretty lost. Many of them had their hearts in the right place, but they just had not yet made the behavioral transition from knucklehead college student to "Professional Leader of Infantrymen."

The West Point guys were out of control. They behaved as if

they'd all just been released from prison. All they cared about was beer and chicks. Sure, at our age we all had a fondness for beer and chicks, but we were supposed to be there answering a higher calling. We were to become Infantry Officers. We were, I felt strongly, under some kind of sacred obligation to take our Infantry Officer training with absolute seriousness. Beer and chicks needed to largely go on standby for a little while.

In retrospect, I might have been wired a bit too tight.

The cadre officer, a captain, decided that his squared away OCS kids were the key to getting his platoon of students to behave. So he made me the Platoon Leader and Eby the Platoon Sergeant.

Leading your peers is always difficult and I wasn't very good at it. However, the damned captain liked the fact that I kept everyone on a short leash. I was determined to do my best to encourage everyone to behave like an eager and competent young officer. Which, of course, drove my peers crazy.

To my horror, instead of changing out platoon leadership every two weeks, the damned cadre captain kept Eby and I in charge of the platoon for almost the entire five months of the course. A number of things made this a particularly difficult time. Infantry Officer Basic was really a terrible course. It was run by cadre that didn't give a shit, the quality of classroom training was farcical and the field training not much better. If the training had been good, it would have been a helova lot easier to lead the platoon because we'd have been doing something that we could take seriously. The training was a joke. The instructors simply stood up in front of the class and ran through Powerpoint slides of largely useless information. The curriculum was an embarrassment, and most of the cadre officers seemed sad, sloppy, and didn't seem to give a shit about passing on skills nor imprinting professional behavior upon us malleable youngsters.

As Platoon Leader, I put a lot of pressure on the guys to be reliable and do what they needed to for us all to succeed. Some of the ways I applied that pressure were pretty ham-handed. I was terribly serious about becoming an Infantry Officer, but I was trying to lead folks that didn't share that seriousness. My solution was not to "adjust my expectations", but to become a tyrant. That created a lot of unhappy lieutenants. They were unhappy with me, and god knows I was damned unhappy with them. I didn't have it in me to lighten up, however. I felt a huge obligation to help them become the serious, tough, and competent Infantry officers that I imagined was our common goal. If this made them hate me, then that would be my cross to bear.

Through all of this angst and turmoil, Warren Eby was my right-hand man. He was utterly reliable, dedicated, disciplined, and competent. In every way, the guy had my back at all times. Nothing got Eby down. He helped lead the platoon through foolishness, inclement weather, and mindless training evolutions with a quiet resolve that buoyed everyone. Day after day I struggled to get the lieutenants in the platoon to show up at the right place at the right time, be in the correct uniform, have the gear they were supposed to bring, and in generally take Infantry School seriously. Eby had the same high expectations for the lieutenants, and did his level best to help the group succeed. He was a fabulous role model for the platoon. Without Eby's unfailing support, the frustrations would have made me crazy. Warren Eby was the best buddy a guy could ever have.

Upon graduation from Infantry School, I knew that Eby and I were to be in the same Ranger class of ~600 that summer of 1989. In a Ranger class, at the beginning, there are three companies of about 200 each. Each company is organized into three platoons of ~65 ea. Each platoon has three squads of ~22. Attrition drops these numbers rapidly.

Your Ranger Buddy is your constant companion. Everywhere you go, he is by your side. Chow, shower, toilet, no matter what you're doing, he must be by your side. If you can't reach out and touch your Ranger Buddy, you're wrong. The usual penalty for failing to stay near your Ranger Buddy was to be tied to him with a three foot cord for a couple days, which is a real pain in the ass.

All I wanted in the world was for Warren Eby to be my Ranger Buddy. Eby was hard as woodpecker lips, strong as a gorilla, tenacious and reliable as a big oak. He was totally unflappable and thoroughly competent. I saw him as the perfect Infantry 2LT and the ideal Ranger Buddy. Out of 600 folks, however, it seemed pretty damned unlikely that Eby and I would be paired up.

Eby brought out the very best in me. I'd never known him to display the slightest sign of weakness. No matter how shitty the conditions had been in the past year, he'd never complained. When I was covered in frost on a 20deg morning and freezing my ass off in my useless Army jacket, it was me complaining about the cold, not him. He'd just shrug. Like, he was acknowledging that he'd heard me, he just hadn't noticed that it was freezing cold. Or when we'd spent the last several hours in a cold rain, standing in a fighting position filled with cold water up to our dicks, it was me that bitched, not him. He never complained.

Standing next to Warren Eby, I could marshal the tenacity and self discipline to get though anything. Eby made whomever stood next to him, a stronger person.

Within minutes of Ranger School's first formation, Eby and I were assigned to the same Company of ~200. That was cool, but nothing to get worked up about. Then Eby and I were assigned to the same Platoon of ~65 within the Company. Now that was really cool. I was starting to hope. 598:1 to 64:1 was a helova improvement.

Then we were assigned to the same Squad!! Holy Shit!! Hearing "pick a Ranger Buddy", I casually walked over to Eby, while inside I was jumping up and down, waving my arms and shrieking with delight. Eby operated within a narrow emotional range, though, so it'd been a terrible faux paus to give him a big hug. With a neutral facial expression, I showed my delight with a he-man sort of eye-contact-with-subtle-nod that said "ok."

City Week. We got a lot of exercise during that first week of Ranger. Georgia in early June is hot and humid. Your sweat doesn't cool you down because it doesn't evaporate. The lack of evaporative cooling means you continue to sweat full-blast. But, as long as you are used to drinking lots of water and sweating it out, it's not a big deal. On the average day we'd do an Army PT (Physical Training) Test, then we'd do calisthenics for a couple hours, then run. Then there'd be obstacle courses, ruck marches, land navigation practice, more PT and running around, hand to hand combat instruction a couple times, etc. We were on the go from well before dawn until about midnight each night. We'd get back to the barracks, shower, square away our gear for the next day, get a couple hours rack time, and it was back at it well before dawn.

Eby was a fit guy. Lean and probably 6' 2", with the broad shoulders. He looked like someone from your college rowing team. He came from the rainy half of Washington State, however, which was no preparation for 18hrs/day of PT in the humid Georgia heat. After a couple days of the City Week PT experience, Eby was starting to slow down. After a grueling day of seemingly non-stop PT, running, and obstacle courses, he turned to me and said "Gress. I'm done."

Me: "Huh?"

"I have to drop out. I can't take this heat. I've not eaten in 2 days, and now I can't keep fluids down. I keep throwing them back up."

I was totally blindsided by this. I frantically cast about for some way I might help. But all I could say was "Dude, oh no."

"I'm sorry. If I keep going like this, I die. I've got to stop and get some fluids in me."

He'd not mentioned any of this to me in the previous days.

Warren Eby had a reservoir of toughness to draw upon that made me look like a mewling kitten.

Eby turned away from me and walked to the nearest Ranger Instructor. There was a brief exchange, the Instructor pointed to the ambulance, and Eby walked away.

I stood there pole-axed with my mouth open and eyes wide with shock. Eby had been one of the greatest, most influential and loyal friends I'd ever had. I'd known him less than a year, but I admired him more than anyone I'd ever met. He was what I wanted to be. I'd have done anything in this world for him. I owed him so much. His incredibly stoic approach to our trials gave me an example to live up to day after day. I've never been so happy in my life as when it became clear that Eby would be my Ranger Buddy. I loved the guy.

I stood there in in the baking heat, in camouflage utilities so soaked with sweat they looked like I'd just emerged from a lake. Tears streamed down my face.

I never saw Warren Eby again. Not ever. In the years that followed, he resisted attempts to stay in touch. I think that dropping out of Ranger School crushed him, and I was too much of a reminder of that failure.

PT Test failure.
As soon as I left the Marines and joined the Army, I started having problems with the lowest bidder Army shorts wearing holes in my inner thighs. They'd get so torn up in a run that they'd start bleeding. The chafing plagued me in both OCS and also Infantry Basic until I started wearing a pair of lycra shorts under the crappy Army shorts. In Ranger School the

concealed lycra shorts got me in big trouble.

We were doing the final Army PT Test. This was City Week, the first 7-10days of Ranger. We'd been doing the damned PT Test every morning, but this was the one that actually meant something. We had to pass. Lol, had to "pass." <rolls eyes>

PT had long been a hobby. The Army doesn't really see the PT test as a competition but the Marines most certainly do. For 7yrs I'd trained hard to "win" every PT test. This day, all I had to do was "pass."

I wasn't sure that Ranger School was going to bother to determine a PT Test "Winner", but I figured that I might as well make an effort to crush everyone in the pushups and situps, and then smoke everyone in the 2mil run. Who knows, maybe I'd get something out of it.

It went poorly.

I barely passed pushups. They kept disqualifying my perfectly acceptable, textbook even, pushups. I was a master of the Army pushup. I could quote the Army standard verbatim, I was perfectly competent at making them Hollywood perfect, and I knew every possible way to execute imperfect pushups that would conserve strength yet most evaluators found to be acceptable. In the Ranger PT Test, I was knocking out Hollywood perfect pushups, but the Ranger Instructor just kept saying the same # over and over again. I understood that they were just trying to add stress, but it was hard to not to be outraged. My pushups were fucking perfect, what the fuck did he want? I had not seen this coming, so I had no plan better then keeping at it and hoping for the best. I'm sure that I did over 110 pushups before I was credited with a passing count of 40. It was really quite irritating.

It was the situps that went awry. The Ranger Instructor spotted my gray lycra shorts that were pulled up under my gray Army shorts. He called some peers over and there was a lot of yelling, wild gesticulating, and spittle flying. It was hard to take the ass-chewing seriously because who could possible give a shit that someone was wearing something a little different, and no more visible, than tighty-whities. The Ranger Cadre failed my situps for "being out of uniform"

It took me a little while to understand just how much trouble I was in. I'd assumed that this was just one more screaming tirade to be endured stoically, with occasional earnest exclamations as seemed appropriate. I'd been thru USMC boot camp and Army OCS. I'd become pretty much impervious to being screamed at. I'd had authority figures in my face screaming at me so many times that I had to tell myself "Don't look bored and roll your eyes."

It seemed though, that there was to be more consequences then just screaming. The Ranger Instructors told me that I was a PT Test failure. I'd just gotten a bunch of demerits, whatever those were, and that meant I was going to be a City Week recycle. That is to say, I'd fail City Week and hope they allowed me to wait around and maybe try again when the next Ranger Class starts in a couple weeks. "This is bad", I fretted.

Next up in the Army PT Test was the 2mile run. I'd been pretty serious about running for a long time. So I figured that unless there was some other intercollegiate runner in the group, I'd be able to win the run and get myself off of this "mystery demerits" shitlist.

I did win the run. However, it wasn't clear that anyone even noticed. When I crossed the finish line with the second finisher so far back that he wasn't even visible, I expected some Ranger Instructor to say "good job" . In the Marines, it was a big deal to win a PT Test run. The fact that no one seemed to care who won the Army PT Test run was worrisome.

My immediate problem was that it seemed that I was still a PT Test failure. That meant trouble. I'd failed a task required to get beyond City Week. Personally, this really had the halmark of being a disaster. Also, I couldn't help but be perplexed that the cadre of this elite organization only cared about passing a *minimum* standard. Never in my life had I cared about a "minimum standard" for anything. "Does this orientation on the minimum standard tell me something about the Army?" I wondered.

I had no idea what I was going to do about the PT Test failure demerits. No one had explained them. Did the demerits mean recycling City Week was a maybe or a certainty? Was there a way to work demerits off? However, I knew better than to ask about something that I wanted to disappear. The simple act of asking about the demerits could make "the system" suddenly remember, "Hey, this kid was supposed to have demerits." I resolved to be very alert, in the coming days, for any mention of demerits. Maybe, I considered, I might find a back-channel way to get an explanation.

The 10mile roadmarch.
I've seen this particular event in the news several times over the years. The average media type can't write about Ranger School. They have no personal life experience of something so difficult, and therefore no context. The reason this particular event is often referenced by the media to illustrate the rigors of the school, is that the media types feel that they can imagine it. The writer breathlessly describes how the Ranger Candidates must walk a whole 10 miles with 40 pounds on their back, as if that's challenging. The total load was actually around 60 pounds, which still isn't much.

What the writers don't understand is that the pace of the 10mi roadmarch is a jog. You're just not allowed to jog. You have to race-walk it.

The easiest way to fail the roadmarch was too many warnings re. jogging. The problem was that you had to jog because the pace was so damned fast. There was a Ranger Instructor bringing up the rear of the group. If you fell back to him for more than a moment or two, he would say "Ranger, you are a

Roadmarch fail. Get in the truck." Within a couple hours you would be settled into the Recycle Barracks and in a couple weeks you'd have one more chance.

In order to walk fast enough to "not quite keep up" you had to move your legs in a race-walk blurring stride that was very hard to maintain. Because the impossibly fast walk wasn't quite fast enough, when Ranger Instructor seemed to be looking, we would jog a half-dozen strides and recover the lost ground. This was much harder for the shorter guys. I don't know how they did it.

The way to succeed was to stay masked from the Ranger Instructors in the group. You had to maintain situational awareness of the location of each Ranger Instructor near you, and what they were looking at one moment to the next. The instant you weren't being observed, you had to make a handful of running strides to make up the distance you'd lost in the last few heartbeats. If you found yourself in an area of near constant observation, you innocently repositioned yourself. Whenever a Ranger Instructor looked right, four to six highly vigilant candidates on the left would run forward a few strides. Conversely for the right side. No planning, no communication nor coordination. Just hundreds of motivated hard-chargers figuring out how to overcome the obstacles.

It would have been a helova lot easier if we'd have been allowed to run the damned ten miles. Having to race-walk it was rough.

The saga of Day Land Navigation.
The Land Nav Tests consisted of being given some points on a map, then you have to go find those points out in the woods and rolling hills. Each point was marked by a small dilapidated sign, often half hidden in the brush, and from it dangled a unique paper "punch." You'd use the punch to put a hole in the appropriate place of your "Land Nav Worksheet" to prove that you'd found the point. Each point was a mile or two from each other. Eight points for Day Land Nav, and six for Night. My

recollection is that we had eight hours to complete each. Since problems were inevitable, you needed to hustle though the heavy vegetation.

Day Land Nav Test. After the usual morning of PTing us half to extinction, we were briefly fed, and then put in tired ill-maintained buses and moved out into the woods via the usual unimproved roads with ruts and holes large enough to swallow a car. We were then put into some old wood and rust bleachers that creaked, swayed, and put slivers in our butts.

It was mid-morning and already hot and humid. A Ranger Instructor stepped away from the other instructors, positioned himself in front of us, got our attention, and began his spiel. We'd all done the Land Nav course a couple times, so we knew the drill. What really got my attention though was that the instructor mentioned that the first of us that got all of his points and got back to the laager site would get some kind of attaboys, and that those would erase demerits. My ears perked up like bat-ears. "Holy shit", I thought, "If I win it erases demerits? Christ almighty this might save my ass." As far as I knew, I'd already failed City Week. I had been going through day after difficult day worrying that, at any moment, my name would be called out and I'd be told to pack my gear.

There was no way that I was the best navigator in the group of 600, but this wasn't really a test of "best navigator". This was a test of "fastest to find all points", and that I might be able to do. I needed to be the fastest runner under hot and humid conditions. In terms of the actual navigation, finding my points out in the woods, I just had to temper my pace enough that I didn't screw up the navigation. I had to be the first of ~600 folks to get back to the laager site, but if one of the "punches" in my Land Nav Worksheet was wrong, I was fucked.

I'd been running intercollegiate or on the college triathlon team for my entire eight year college tour. Of the sprinkling of intercollegiate runners in the military, chances were that none of them were there in the woods with me. The pressure was on. According to what the Ranger Instructor said, a win in Day Land Nav would clear up half of the demerits that were hanging over my neck. I kept telling myself "you can do this. Haul ass. Don't screw up. Haul ass. Don't screw up."

I rec'd my Land Nav Worksheet that had a map section and a list of my points as defined by 8 digit "grid coordinates." I plotted the coordinates on the map with a fine 0.5mm pencil, double-checked my plotting, and made a judgment call re. the logical sequence of points to hit.

The trick to navigating accurately and in a big hurry is to find some recognizable terrain feature near your target point. A hilltop, a saddle, a fork in a creek, anything that you think that you can find in the woods pretty easily. This is called a "Tack Point."

By heading for an obvious tack point, instead of a half-visible signpost, it was a lot harder to screw up. That let me concentration on hauling ass instead of slowly and meticulously following an azimuth or pace count for fear that if I was off by a little bit, I might be screwed. Imagine, for example, the situation if you travel two miles through the woods only to end up equi-distant from two signs 150 yards apart.

Once I found my tack point, I'd shoot another azimuth for the supposed direction to the nearby signpost, and run the plotted distance. If I didn't see the signpost immediately, I'd start a rectangular search pattern until I found the darn thing. Sometimes you had to bump into the signpost to find it.

With the first tack point chosen, I used a protractor to get my first compass vector and carefully put my map into a ziplock bag to protect it. With compass in one hand and rifle in the other, I headed out of the laager site at a run. It was damned hot, but I had 2 canteens on me, and each nav point was supposed to have water at it.

Following my compass azimuth and keeping my "running pace count" in my head I jogged thru the woods, over bushes and felled trees, I found my first point a mile or two away. I was totally soaked with sweat. Anxious to hustle, I quickly drank down a canteen and refilled it from the water jug at the navigation point. Then I pulled the Land Nav Worksheet out of its bag, being careful not to drip sweat on it, and used the punch device tied to the signpost to punch a hole in my worksheet at the appropriate location. Once again, on the map, I identified a tack point near the next sign post that I had to find a mile or two distant. I used the protractor to get a compass azimuth to the tack point, estimated distance, put the map away, grabbed my rifle and jogged off through the woods, compass in hand, and keeping track of my running pace count.

I got to the tack point, and repeated the above process to find the second and third navigation points. At each Nav Point, I'd drink down one of my quart canteens, fill it back up from the Nav Point's water jugs, and figure out how to get to the next point.

I'd been running in the Southern California heat for eight years. As long as I kept drinking water, I figured I could run in the heat all day.

At the fourth point there wasn't enough water left to completely refill my canteen. At the fifth point there was no water. There were a couple guys sitting down and resting, drenched in sweat. At the sixth point there were more guys, some sitting, some sprawled, all drenched in sweat.

There were probably a hundred navigation points set up out there in the woods, but each of us only had eight points to find. Each point had a unique paper punch, so when we returned the Ranger Instructors would check the paper punches on our worksheet against some key.

How we got to each point was up to us. Since there were ~600 of us, any one of my points was probably shared by fifty other guys. What route each of us took to get to our points, and therefore the sequence with which we got to the points, was up to us. So altho this was the sixth point in the scheme I chose as the most efficient way to get to all my points, it could have been the first point or the eight point for other guys. I had no way of knowing.

At my seventh point there were guys crapped out in the shade and some were asking newcomers if they had water. At my eigth point, there were lots of guys sprawled about. There was no talking, they just kinda laid there with their mouths open. They didn't look too good.

With eight punches on my Land Nav Worksheet, I was done. There was no way for me to know if someone had already got their eight points. Certainy there had to be some of us that, as luck would have it, got points that were close together. All I could do now was run like hell for the laager site. If I fucked up any of my points, it was too late to fix that. I had about four miles that I needed to run, so all I could do is maintain my best possible pace for four miles in full uniform, load bearing vest, and carrying my weapon. I'd been running through the woods for almost four hours. I'd drank around two gallons of water. I was drenched with sweat it was coming out of my boot-tops.

We weren't allowed to be on the dirt roads that were in the area unless we had found all our points and were heading back to the laager site. There were supposed to be Ranger Instructors walking the dirt roads to catch us if we broke this rule, so I'd not dared to use the dirt roads while looking for my points. Now that I was done, howeer, I was free to use the dirt roads. Even though they were not the most direct route, I could run a lot faster on a road then trying to "break brush" through the woods. I headed for the logical road that would get me to the laager site.

It took about a half mile to get to the road. Once there, I turned and really started hauling ass for the finish, a couple miles away. There'd been no obvious goatscrews, so I'd found all my points pretty efficiently. I'd gone hard the whole way. As long as I didn't screw up one of my points, I had a chance to win this, I figured. I really needed those attaboys. If someone even beat me my a couple seconds, I was fucked. I ran down the dirt road for the distant laager site at the fastest pace I could sustain.

En route, I passed a lot of guys crapped out in the shaded ditches at the sides of the dirt road. It looked like the heat had done them in. The military expression is "the dying cockroach." Since they weren't supposed to be on the road, I guessed that they'd decided that they needed help more than they needed to finish Day Land Nav. That got my attention because the idea of "I'm messed up so I'm going to stop" isn't something one hears too often in Ranger School, short of imminent death. I ran on, hard as I could maintain.

Eventually I got to the laager site. As I brought my pace down to a jog and then a walk, I left a trail of moisture in my wake as if I'd stepped out of a pool. The instructors seemed a little alarmed at my apparent fluid loss and pointed me towards some water jugs so that I might refill my canteens. I carefully took my map out of its ziplock bag and handed it to an instructor that seemed to want it. He confirmed that my punch marks were correct and exclaimed "Congratulations Ranger, you're the first one back."

I was briefly overwhelmed by the thought of "Thank god". Then I said, "Ahh, the reason I'm first is that everyone else is doing the dying cockroach out there. Both on the sides of the road, and at the nav points. They ran out of water a long time ago." There was silence. Then things got busy. Instructors jumped into vehicles. Radios called for ambulances, vehicles roared off, and within a couple minutes I was practically alone.

I drank down my canteens, refilled and drank them down again. I sat down and leaned against a tree. It was quite peaceful. No one was making me do anything. I was pretty tired, but it had been a good day. I'd earned back half of my demerits. I closed my eyes, luxuriated in the knowledge that "there's nothing I have to do right now", and took a nap.

Night Land Nav.

Night Land Nav is pretty damned difficult. What makes it so hard is, stating the obvious, you can't goddamned see. We were allowed to use flashlights with a red lens. Crappy Army flashlights don't put out much illumination on their best day, but with a red lens, it's more of a "glow" then something you can use to find your way in heavy vegetation.

Everything you take for granted navigating during the day becomes a helova lot harder at night. You can't use tack points because most terrain features short of a cliff or a river just aren't that obvious when you can't see spit. A broad hilltop or a saddle is undistinguishable from its surroundings if your ability to sense terrain changes is limited to a vague horizonless sense of "am I going uphill or downhill?" Miss your terrain feature by 100m and you'll be way off when you try to "tack" to the location of the "nearby" signpost. You'd spend an hour stumbling around a 100m square with your glowing red lens trying to find the signpost in the bushes. Then you'd lose confidence that you'd correctly found the terrain feature, or you'd get disoriented doing the grid search for the sign. Then your only recourse would be to find your way back to the previous nav point and try all over again. At that point, best case you'd have pissed away 2hrs. Worst case, you were on your way to end up a pile of sun-bleached and gnawed bones for archeologists to pick through later.

At night, it's hard to dogleg around the impassible <whatever>. If you get to a serious gully or are faced with vegetation so thick that you can't get thru, you have to find a way around the obstacle that leaves you on azimuth and with an intact pace count. But if you can't see anything, it's really hard to make a precise ½ circle around something the size of a city block. Once on the other side you have to position yourself accurately so your original azimuth and adjusted pace count will get you to the barely visible signpost. Heck, just try to make a perfect 200m half circle blindfolded.

At night it's hard to move quickly. You constantly run into obstacles that you can't bull through and you inevitably attempt to go the wrong way around the largely invisible obstacle. Also, you could be fighting your way thru very difficult vegetation, having no idea that there is a relatively clear path 10m away.

At night you can't shoot long azimuths with your compass. There's no sighting in on a tree 400yds away and then running to it. The glowing red lens is good for only a couple feet.

At night it's hard to find the signposts. They aren't reflective. If you're not close enough to touch the damned thing, you're not going to see it.

I didn't have much experience with Night Land Nav, but I really needed those attaboys. I was worried. I won Day Land Nav because I was a runner. But the heat wasn't going to slow folks down much in the middle of the night. I couldn't run thru the woods if visibility was limited to 2' because all I had was the sorry glow from a POS Army flashlight and its red lens. The very things that gave me an edge in Day Land Nav weren't looking to be much help at night. I worried, "how the hell does being the best runner get a blind guy thru the Land Nav course the fastest?" It was tempting to just "hope", but goddamnit, this was important. I needed a plan.

An idea started to form. It was June. The days were pretty darn long. Night Land Nav consisted of only 6 points not the 8 that we had during the day, and the points were a bit closer together. .

At the laager site, waiting anxiously for the Land Nav Worksheets to get handed out, I watched the available light that I so desperately needed, recede. With little light left, we finally got our Land Nav Worksheets with maps eight digit points to be plotted. Using my red lens flashlight I carefully plotted my points, rechecked them, and organized them into a logical sequence. I used my protractor to get my first azimuth and distance, and I headed out. Just as fast as I could go. No sustainable jog this time. I was racing the end of gray twilight. I kept my red lens flashlight off so I would retain every bit of night vision I could.

I figured that I had about 30min worth of failing illumination before it was pitch dark under the tall trees. My plan was to race at full speed to the 5 closest points while I still had a little illumination. That way, once I couldn't see anything, I would have only a single point or two of genuine "struggle in the inky darkness."

I charged thru the woods on my azimuth and kept a pace count. I could see a little. Because the points weren't as far apart as Day Land Nav, I didn't bother with tack points. I simply ran on my azimuth and pace count directly for the distant nav point sign. I compensated for diversions around big obstacles as best I could.

I found the first point in less than ten minutes of running hard cross country, and used the hanging paper punch on my map sheet. I turned on my red light, pulled out my protractor and identified the next azimuth and distance. It wasn't very far away. Then I turned my light back off to save night vision, and headed out at a run. It only took ten minutes to find the second point in the fading light. The third nav point was a little farther away, but I did the absolute best I could with keeping up a fast pace thru the woods in what little light still remained. In twenty minutes I was standing at my third nav point and working out the azimuth and distance for the fourth point.

The fourth point was a struggle. I got to the area quickly enough, but I had to do a grid search with my red light in the now inky darkness to find the damned sign post. With the fourth point found, I'd run out of daylight but I'd knocked out four of the six points. Now, I had only two points to find in total dark. For the first time that evening, I paused, drank down a canteen and refilled it from a water jug at the signpost.

With my protractor, I got the azimuth to the fifth point, estimated distance, and headed out, this time with my red lens flashlight in one hand and compass in the other. It was rough going. The vegetation was intermittently pretty thick and since I couldn't take a compass sighting on something distant, I had to have my head down looking at my glowing compass a lot. I was worried that if I tried to work my way around heavy vegetation, that I'd fall off of the compass azimuth and I'd be hosed. So, as best I could, I bulled my way thru the brush.

I took a beating. With my head down watching the compass, my face ran smack into every damned stick, branch and prickly-bush. I tried to use my cap visor to protect my eyes as best I could. My face got chewed up a bit.

When I got to the area where I estimated the fifth signpost to be, I could see the red glow of other Ranger Candidates. It turned out that these guys were at the sign post plotting their next move. It was probably their second or third nav point, not their fifth, because they had likely been far more deliberate in getting to their first points.

Realizing how helpful it was to have a red glow at each nav point, I looked carefully at each person at the sign post to confirm that they were all candidates like me. Then I whispered to the group. "Tell everyone that when they get to a signpost, to face outboard with their red lights as they figure out their next azimuth. Your lights guided me in. Keep doing that and we can guide lots of guys to their nav points."

Everyone seemed to think that this is was a great idea. Ranger School is a highly cooperative affair, not a competition. We were all in this together and happy to help each other out.

My fifth point found and nav worksheet punched, I used my protractor to ID my last azimuth and estimated the distance. I also looked to see the best way to get from that point back to the laager site. Once again, I'd head from my last point directly to the nearest road that would take me in the right direction. By figuring this out now, I thought I could just punch my nav worksheet at the sixth point and immediately head for the road without having to pause.

I left the group and headed out on my azimuth. Now that I realized that there were almost sure to be Ranger Candidates standing around the point with their lights on, I figured that I just had to get close to the point. That meant that I could move faster and accept some risk that my azimuth and pace count wouldn't be exactly right. I didn't have to keep my head glued to the glowing compass for fear of going astray because of the lack of visual reference points in the woods. I didn't have to worry about ending up 100m off my destination and struggling with a desperate grid search to find a half-hidden signpost in the now inky darkness. I just needed to get to the general vicinity as fast as I could.

Now that I could keep my eyes up, I was able to move pretty fast.

Sure enough, as I neared the site where my pace count indicated the signpost should be, I could suddenly see a red glow off to one side. I hustled over to the group and used the hole punch on my nav worksheet. Once again I quietly mentioned the idea of letting plenty of red light spill out when they were at a nav point, and asked them to pass the word.

Then I pulled out the compass and headed out roughly in the direction of the road as fast as the vegetation and the red glow would allow. I didn't have to be all that accurate, there was no way I was going to miss that road. Once I got to the road, I turned and ran like hell for the laager site a couple miles away.

When I got to the laager site, the Ranger Instructors were hanging around near a fire joking and laughing. I got the impression they didn't expect anyone back for a while yet.

They weren't yet set up to check out the punch holes in the nav worksheets, and didn't have the water jugs pulled out of the trucks. Me showing up mostly just caused confusion.

Some Ranger Instructor (RI), in kindly but puzzled tone: "Who are you?"

"Ranger Gress, SGT."

RI: "Aren't you supposed to be out there on the land nav course? You having trouble?"

"I found my points SGT. I think I'm done."

<pause as the group of instructors register that some kid has come in prematurely yet says he's done>
RI: "You've got all 6 points?"

"Yes SGT."

RI: "Well, ok, lets find the answer key then."

A couple minutes later it was "What did you say your name was?"

"Ranger Gress, SGT"

RI: "Are you the same Ranger that won Day Land Nav."

"Yes SGT."

RI: "Well, you can navigate, I'll give you that. Go wash your face, you're bleeding all over on my Land Nav course."

I restrained my normally irresistible inclination to attempt a one-liner. It was not a culture that is amused by frivolous comments.

Once again I was the first one done with Land Nav. By getting most of my points while there was enough ambient light to run like hell, I'd completed the course with hours yet left available. I breathed a huge sigh of relief. As long as I didn't screw up again, I was good to get thru City Week. The Recycle sword was no longer poised over my throat. Thank god.

In the weeks that followed I spent 100's of hours on patrols with guys that had come to Ranger School from the Ranger Battalions. In addition to being the most motivated, the most competent, and the mentally hardest group among us, some of them were truly incredible navigators. Several times one of them would recognize some subtle terrain feature nearby and mention that we'd been in this area before. For example, one day I was "taking a knee" in a hasty halt next to one of them, and he pointed to some nearby insignificant draw running up the side of the ridge. He whispered, "see that draw? This is the same place we moved thru 5 days ago. We just came through from over there" pointing off in some direction.

My brain's gears whirred and I thought back to the previous missions and the painstaking terrain models that I'd created for each mission brief. I try to place that inconsequential draw along the route of a previous mission. I had carefully marked those routes on those terrain models that I'd sculpted with exquisite care to show even the most subtle of terrain features. And I couldn't do what he just did. I was worn out from the constant physical exertion, I hadn't slept more than an hour/night in weeks, and I was starving. I did not have a good enough memory for terrain and our movement routes to remember that damned subtle little draw. But those guys could. They were really studs. I was just a runner.

Obstacle and Confidence Courses.
I wasn't much good at the obstacle courses. It helped that I was fit and a little taller than average, but I've never been very coordinated and I don't like heights very much. I wouldn't want to admit being scared of heights, I like to think of it more along the lines of having legitimate concerns.

There were a number of training evolutions that had us climbing or hanging way up off the ground. Trying very hard not to die, I was a bit slower than average at all of this. Sometimes we were so damned exhausted that we had very little grip strength in our hands left. Everything we had to hang on to, suspended way up in the air, was slippery. There were a number of times when I was hanging way off the ground suspended only by my fingers gripping some pole polished smooth and oiled by thousands of other hands over the years. One had to really have their wits about them and look for places to grab that had a knot or other surface imperfection that would allow your fingers some purchase. There were many times when I was scared shitless because my damn fingers were slipping and the fall was going to break my damn legs. The various obstacle and confidence courses seemed to put me in one life-threatening "holy shit I'm about to fall to my death" emergency after another. Repeatedly almost falling to my death was a source of some stress.

Being a little taller is a big deal in obstacle and confidence courses because there's an awful lot of reaching up and climbing over things. The Stairway To Heaven, pictured below, was just one example of the many demonic perils.

Stairway to Heaven. Common military obstacle. This particular obstacle is at Marine Corps Recruit Depot, San Diego. During the summer of 1982, I climbed up and over that obstacle probably dozen times, but never happily. (DOD)

 It goes up into the air really high, I don't know, maybe four stories. As you move up, the logs get farther apart. They are also worn very smooth by thousands of oily hands. About half way up you have to perch on one log to get to the next. If you miss your grab, you over-balance and fall to your death. When you get near the top, you have to stand on one log to get to the next. It is really quiet terrifying.

Obstacles like this caused in me a degree of "legitimate concern" that was darn near paralyzing. But it had to be done or I would be a failure. So I gritted my teeth, made myself focus on the task with laser-beam intensity, and I slowly and methodically made my way up, over the top log, and then down. I took great care to never look down at the ground. I stayed focused on the log I needed to hang on to.

Sure, I'd done this obstacle a number of times over the years, but being acquainted with it didn't make it suck any less.

The fact that we were all exhausted made the obstacles much harder. Also, almost all the obstacles, and there were lots of different kinds, were tougher on short guys. Things I might be able to get up on my toes and grab, a shorter guy would have to leap for. Either he'd get a good grab on the <whatever> above the first time, or he'd plummet to Earth. Those shorter guys had balls of steel.

I had mentioned that of the 48 Infantry Lieutenants that started Ranger School with me, only one other guy earned his Ranger Tab. That other guy was one of those short guys with balls of steel. He couldn't have been over five foot, six inches, but he was one hard dude.

The saga of the Close Combat Pit.
We'd been to the close combat pit, a ~30m diameter circle of woodchips, a couple times already. Theoretically we were learning close combat techniques, but since it takes hundreds of hours to really gain any martial arts skills, this was mostly just another way to wear us down.

It was around 11PM. We were exhausted. The ~550 of us, we'd already lost around fifty, had made it through six days of City Week, but we were pretty much at the end of our strength. The eighteen hour days of calisthenics, daily PT Tests, obstacle courses, road marches, land nav and the heat stress, had plumb worn us out.

Like we had been told, later, we would indeed remember fondly City Week's honest three hours of sleep per night and two solid meals per day.

Close combat drill in the pit was unloved. There was no escaping the wood chips that would immediately get under our clothing the first time one went rolling across the ground. The woodchips would stick to our soaking wet uniforms as if we'd been tarred and feathered. Our clothes would take days to completely free themselves of woodchips. Until then, they itched. Getting the woodchips off of our skin turned even an ice-cold shower into heaven-sent relief from the inescapable itching that threatened one's sanity. We really hated those woodchips. Of course, you couldn't say that in public. That would be an admission of weakness. Behind the stoic facade I worked hard to maintain, however, I had a special quiet place of loathing for rolling around in woodchips.

We were all so exhausted that we couldn't really execute the judo throws that we were being directed to practice. We were weak as kittens. We got yelled at a lot for our lack of aggressiveness, but we could hardly stand.

The Ranger Instructors started threatening various unhappy outcomes if we didn't start showing some moxie. Imagine that you're so tired that in order to stay upright you and your sparring partner often lean against each other. Your balance is shaky. It takes help from your buddy just to get back up on your feet. Then someone yells "IF YOU GIRLS DON'T START SHOWING ME JUDO THROWS LIKE YOU'VE GOT A PAIR, WE'RE GOING TO BE HERE UNTIL DAWN. THAT'S OK. I'VE GOT ALL NIGHT.

Somehow we all figured out that with a bit of cooperative buddy-aid, we could create the appearance of executing the judo throws well enough to mollify our tormentors. It was a matter of the "throwee" kinda collapsing over the "thrower's" shoulder and doing a perfectly timed largely invisible "hop" to go up and over the throwers shoulder to end up rolling across the woodchips. The throwee didn't actually do much throwing, it was all in the hop. But in the middle of the night and with only the dim illumination of a few street lights I suppose that it appeared that the thrower was executing a judo throw. In reality, the exhausted thrower barely exerted himself.

For the next hour the ~550 of us refined this technique of "hop and roll" and the Ranger Instructors berated us less. We moved as slow as we could. We figured out the apparent threshold of beratement, and we did as little as possible. All we were really interested in was showering off all the damned woodchips and collapsing for some rest.

Then 6-7 HMMWV ambulances pulled up. The 550 of us looked at them warily. Medics were not our friends. Spend 24hrs away from training due to some medical issue, real or imagined, and it's an automatic recycle.

One unguarded complaint to a Medic during Ranger School, and it could be a recycle for you. In the field phases that followed, we didn't let a medic see a problem unless we thought we were in danger of losing a limb. All the medic had to say was something sympathetic like "well, why don't we get you off your feet for a couple hours" and you could end up in the Recycle Barracks. Imagine the horror of recycling the FL swamp phase because you asked a medic for some moleskin to patch a little owie. The "get you off your feet for a little while" could mean you spending some time relaxing at a casualty collection point while the doc fussed over you. All sorts of ways for that to go bad. Your platoon could have easily moved on its next mission, so how do they get you back to it? Or maybe they want you to see a different doc? Or maybe the doc says you need to say off your feet for an overnight. You could take a little nap and all the sudden you're a Recycle. You had to be really careful around medics.

Somewhat visible in the mixed lighting of overhead and headlights, someone from an ambulance was in a debate with one of the Ranger Instructors. We couldn't make out what they were saying but the tone and body language wasn't happy. Then the medic with the boss body language pulled out a bullhorn and said…

"Ok, this shit is going to stop right now. My name is LTC <whatever> of the <whatever> Medical Activity. We had fifty cases of heat stroke and heat exhaustion yesterday." <that

would have been Day Land Nav>

<He turned towards the Ranger Instructors that were grouped together and glaring at him> "That kind of bullshit is going to stop before someone dies. This place is out of control."

<He turned back towards us> "We're here to help. If any of you have the following symptoms, I want you to come over here right now. We'll give you an IV to replace some of those fluids you've been losing. So if any of you feel:
Weak
Nauseous
Light-headed
Exhausted
Dizzy
Sweating profusely
Not sweating enough
Hot and dry skin
Clammy and wet skin

Come over here right now. Give us 30min to get some fluids in you, and then you can go back to training."

He lowered the bullhorn and looked at us expectedly. A disorganized group of a couple dozen medical types had formed up behind him.

The 550 of us all looked at each other in confusion. Of course we all had these symptoms, the only thing that was keeping us upright was an dried salt and woodchips. We were totally exhausted. I didn't know what was going on, but the training environment was very unsympathetic to missing a few hours of training and once in the clutches of medic do-gooders, one lost control of their destiny.

"I think this is a bad idea", I said softly to my judo partner.

"Ya, I ain't doin' it," he mumbled back.

Most of us stayed rooted right there in the woodchips. But about 200 folks saw the glorious opportunity to fucking-just-sit-down-for-god's-sakes, and walked over to the ambulances. Getting a poke in the arm sounded like a small price to pay for being able to sit and rest for a couple minutes.

The Ranger Instructors tried to get things going again, but our heart wasn't in it. We consumed another hour with a few more pathetic throwee assisted judo throws to placate the instructors, then we were done for the night and they marched us back to the barracks.

The next morning, uncharacteristically, a mass formation was called of all three companies, all ~550 of us that had made it thru the past week. This was the last day of City Week. With few exceptions, that would probably find out today, we'd made it. Hopefully the day would mostly just be a matter of shipping out to the other side of Ft. Benning for two weeks of squad patrols in Darby Phase. I was hoping I'd hear some kind of confirmation that my Land Nav efforts had indeed erased the mystery demerits.

Some officer stood up in front of the ~550 of us. He said....."Everyone that got an IV last night, fall out over here <gesturing to his left>.

I mentally implored the 200 "Don't do it, don't do it. He doesn't know who you are. For the love of god, don't move."

~150 folks, maybe 50 short of the real total, moved to the other formation.

The officer then said "Those of you that got IVs last night have to go to the hospital for observation. The medical staff decided that you were all suffering from heat exhaustion. Since you will miss more than 24hrs of training, you will all recycle to the next Ranger Class."

There was stunned silence. I stood there horrified at how close I came to going for last night's sit down and rest party. "

And that is how my Ranger Class put 150 in the hospital for heat stroke/heat exhaustion. We were briefly infamous over that.

Being incompetent.
Every mission started with the "Planning Process", the primary element being the Operations Order (OPORD) that contained every detail about the mission, divided among 5 paragraphs….
Situation
Mission
Execution
Administration and Logistics
Command and Control

Inevitably there would be some Annexes too, a critical one being the Fire Support Annex that addressed the planning of artillery and mortar fire, and also helo gunship and fast-mover assets, if any, with air-to-ground weaponry.

If we were going to do an Air-Mobile helo insertion, or an Airborne parachute insertion, we had guys with experience planning those Annexes.

I, sadly, had very little experience at any of this. I had thought that I was pretty good at the "Planning Process", having just come out of Infantry Officer Basic, but I was wrong. Therefore I had little to contribute to the group effort of writing the Operations Order. Being unskilled at a critical task is a problem. Being unable to contribute to the group working on a critical task is worse. In Ranger School, there's little room for guys that don't have much to contribute.

Ranger School set a pretty high bar for the level of detail needed in the small Infantry unit OPORD, a far higher standard than what had been expected of us in Infantry Officer

Basic. There was a bitter irony there. The very guys that one would expect to be shit-hot at planning small unit Infantry actions, were actually the weak sisters. The other Ranger Candidates had all gone thru preparatory training for Ranger, and that training put a lot of emphasis on the small Infantry Unit OPORD. But Infantry Officer Basic eschewed any kind of special Ranger Prep kind of planning, tactics, and Infantry skills training. Its leadership flattered themselves by imagining that "by our very nature we are the best preparation for Ranger School," when in fact they provided the worst preparation.

Every officer branch, like Infantry, Armor, Artillery, etc. has their own school to train 2LTs. In those schools a smattering of Ranger trained officers conduct special additional training for those young officers that declare a desire to go to Ranger School. In my "very definition of Ranger School preparation" Infantry School, however, none of our cadre officers were Ranger trained. None of them. Zero. Way to put your best foot forward US Army Infantry.

Now, looking back over of 23yrs of military service, I participated in a wide variety of formal military training. Some of it was terrific, but most of it was terrible. The Marines make an effort to staff their entry level school houses, like Bootcamp, OCS, and the first tier of occupational skills programs, with their very best folks. The schoolhouse is often hard duty. In the Marines, if a person's service record says that they spent time as schoolhouse cadre, that means that someone thought that they were a shit-hot Marine. Because, in the Marines, only the best get chosen to spend time with malleable youngsters at the service entry points.

In the Army though, it's a very different dynamic. Because the schoolhouse can be long hours of thankless, ineffective, micromanaged toil, hard charging Army types generally try to avoid it. Every strong subordinate, over time, collects a network of sugar daddies, each of whom remember fondly that really terrific subordinate that they relied upon very much.

When the day comes that hard-charging subordinate gets orders to become schoolhouse cadre, he/she starts calling their sugar daddies for help getting out of the assignment. One of those folks will inevitably say "Heck with that, I want you to come work for me again. I'll make it happen." As a result, the best Army types often manage to avoid the schoolhouse. So if a tour as schoolhouse cadre appears on your service record, that is interpreted as, fairly or not, you didn't impress anyone enough to get you out of that assignment.

Over time the quality of training in the Army schoolhouses gets worse and worse because the low percentage of leaders with really high standards passing thru year after year, allows a culture of mediocrity to penetrate every facet of the training. The few hard chargers that wind up as cadre get their enthusiasm sucked out by the micromanaged rigid mediocrity. Most Army training wouldn't intellectually challenge a turnip. We didn't learn a lot in Infantry Officer Basic.

As a result of our miserable preparation, the 48 Infantry 2nd Lieutenants that started Ranger School with me were the guys least prepared of the ~600 in our class. Some of those ~600 were young enlisted soldiers only a couple years out of bootcamp, but it was us officers fresh out of Infantry Officer Basic that couldn't plan our way out of a paper bag, had poor patrolling skills, and were physically and mentally weak. Sigh.

The Operations Order (OPORD) Planning Process.
Planning a mission and preparing for the mission brief required ~12hrs of total focus. The Platoon Leader would come up with a basic scheme in a couple minutes, and then delegate significant portions of the work to others.

The Plt Ldr, or Sqd Ldr for the squad level missions in Darby Phase, all the other guys involved in creating the OPORD, and all the other folks that were hidden in security positions protecting the site, all had to execute their roles while thoroughly exhausted. The Plt Ldr had to be everywhere because he was responsible for everything. All it would take is for a Listening Post (LP) to fall asleep, while most of us were focused on preparing the OPORD, and the whole chain of command would fail. Failure, like a sword poised over the throat of each leader-of-the-day, usually meant recycling the phase.

By the second daily mission of Darby Phase, the squad had figured out who had particular strengths useful for the planning process. One guy was a wizard with the Fire Support Annex, another guy was a wizard with the long and complicated Execution section, another could rip out the Administration and Logistics, and Command and Control sections like he'd memorized 100's of OPORDS in a previous life. Meanwhile the Sqd Ldr was brainstorming ideas with these folks, making their separate actions synch with each other, and synch with his own scheme. I wasn't much good at any of that, and that was a problem.

If you weren't contributing much, then you weren't of much use to the group. Sure, you could be one of the guys on perimeter security, but if someone had to get Peered, it was those low contribution guys that took the hit. Also, staying awake while lying behind a bush on the perimeter, for hour after hour, was a total horror show. The eternity was spent one unguarded minute away from accidently falling asleep, a crime that could easily lead to washing out. Therefore it was terribly important to have "real job" during the ~8-12hrs each day that the group spent planning the next mission. A real job kept you busy doing something, as opposed to lying behind a bush day-dreaming about food. If your busy doing something, it's easy to stay awake.

Although the other guys looked out for each other pretty obsessively, falling asleep while on security was a special category of crime because it was perceived as a leadership failure. Dozing off for a moment, having not slept in three days, could result in your entire chain of command, squad leader, platoon sergeant, and platoon leader, all failing their evaluations. That could easily mean they all recycle that phase. So if you couldn't be trusted to stay awake, even if the Ranger Instructors didn't catch you, you'd get Peered out.

Desperate for something to do for the OPORD planning process, I tried my hand at making the mission terrain model.

A terrain model is a depiction of the mission area (AO-Area of Operations) in the dirt. For example, if the ground that the mission will have you move over can be drawn on a 4km x 4km map square then in the dirt you could mark off 8x8'. Then with string you could quickly make 16 squares, each 2' on a side, totaling 32 sq ft of ground. In complex terrain you would then spend hours shaping all the terrain in the 32ft^2 with loving detail. You make the high points in the AO at least a foot high so that the terrain model can show lots of vertical detail. In order to portray every nuance of the terrain features, one must study the topographic map of the area very carefully.

A topographical map uses elevation lines to show how the shape of the terrain varies. With some experience, you can extract an incredible amount of detailed information re. the precise shape of the terrain by studying the changing swirls of the topo lines millimeter by millimeter.

A large scale terrain model should show should show every subtle draw, finger, the small changes of slope, and the exact shape of the hills and ridges. The tiniest variation in the map's topo lines should be visible in the changing shape of the terrain model. It's like making a big sculpture, and I became pretty good at it. Once I got the ground laid out, I'd label everything of significance to the mission. Routes, the objective, rally points, everything. Usually I made a separate, much larger, scale model of the objective itself. That gave the leader something to use to brief "actions on the objective."

The second mission brief that used my terrain model won the Squad Leader a "detailed and effective terrain model" comment on his must-pass leadership position eval. I finally had something to contribute to the group, and that helped my standing in the Peer Reviews. In the months that followed we had a mission almost every day. Every leader, upon being shoved into the position, immediately chooses their key people. Every leader chose me to make his terrain model.

Becoming the squad's and later the platoon's terrain model guy, was a big deal for several reasons.

1) All the practice studying topo maps in such excruciating detail made me pretty darn competent at reading topo maps. This became a second competency for me….I'd won Day and Night Land Nav because I was a runner, but now I was learning genuine navigational skills.

2) The guy doing the terrain model ends up with a pretty solid understanding of how the mission will work. This was huge because the leaders that created the mission plan weren't going to be the ones that executed the plan. So at the end of the two hour mission brief, that you spent with your head nodding down on to your chest as sleep tried to take over, you could suddenly become the Platoon Leader responsible for execution. The new leadership team of, Plt Ldr, Plt Sgt, and three Sqd Ldrs, had about 60 seconds to adjust to the idea and then the platoon had to move out to conduct the mission.

In order to get a platoon leader position "Pass", you not only had to be damned squared away, work incredibly hard, but also a lot of stars needed to align in your favor. Lots of competent hard-chargers failed leadership positions, sometimes to no fault of their own. If your understanding of the mission, checking your notes from the briefing, seemed to consist of a few chicken scratches, you were fucked.

Terrain model guy, more so than almost any other person in the platoon, had good retention of a large fraction of the critical mission details. As we moved, hour after hour, along the planned route and executed the mission, I did my part to make the chain of command look good. When it was my turn in one of the leadership positions, everyone did their very best for me.

The Chicken.
Our first "Phase" out in the woods was at Ft. Benning. This was called Darby Phase after Major William O. Darby, arguably the father of the modern US Army Rangers. Darby was our introduction to being constantly wet and exhausted while starving and sleep deprived.

One rainy afternoon the 18man squad was directed to go to a truck and get "dinner", but instead of each being handed an MRE field ration for the day, the squad was instead handed a single scrawny ill-tempered chicken. We all kind of looked at each other in confusion.

We were not, of course, dumb enough to let go of the chicken.

We were then told that the chicken was dinner. For all 18 of us. We had 30min to make it happen.

The squad leader of the day said something along the lines of "do we have any farmboys?" I grew up in little OR/WA logging towns, not farm towns. I had once milked a cow and found it that it was damned hard. I kept my mouth shut.

The squad leader said "Ok, We gotta kill the chicken, we gotta clean it so we can cook it, and we gotta make a fire." He looked at us, apparently seeking volunteers.

I figured that making a fire, standing there in the woods in the rain was impossible. I didn't know anything about cleaning a dead chicken so it could be cooked up. And I certainly didn't want to be the one to kill the poor thing. I kept my mouth shut.

A couple guys said they could make a fire. They saw some kind of wood that burnt even when it was wet. They called it "oil wood" or some other complete bullshit. That they could build a fire in the rain was so ludicrous that I rolled my eyes theatrically. Those guys just didn't to be the ones to kill the chicken.

The rest of us just stood there and looked mournfully at the damned chicken. It's endearing little head movements, while held in someone's arms, were quickly finding a place in our hearts as our new squad mascot. It kept darting its head to look at each of us individually. It looked for all the world like it was saying "hi everyone". We were terribly hungry though. For two weeks we'd burned twice the calories we'd consumed and it was starting to show. We stood in a loose huddle, cold and wet gazed helplessly at "our squad mascot", and felt sorry for ourselves. The chicken was passed around several times with statements like "here. You do it."

We were running out of time. To my complete surprise, a little camp fire was starting up next to the group. In the rain. To this day I don't know how those guys did that. They put a couple canteens of water in the fire.

Finally, hunger and the ticking clock spurred me to action. I ground my teeth in distaste and exclaimed "here, give me the goddamned thing. I'll do it." I reached for our poor scrawny squad mascot, grabbed it by the neck, and with my face twisted up in a grimace, I whipped it around.

"Ok, it's dead."Now what do we do?"

"We gotta take the feathers off and gut it" someone said.

"How do we do that?"

We had about fifteen minutes left. For several minutes we tried haplessly to get the feathers off. Then someone said the feathers would come off if we boiled it. That sounded reasonable.

We cut off the head and feet easily enough. In order to gut the thing we made a large cut across the abdomen and scooped out a bunch of yucky stuff. The amazing fire makers had two canteen cups of tepid water. We had no flat surface to use as a cutting board so we tore the chicken in half more than cut it.

"Into the pot," I said, and we put a handful of bones and chicken feathers into each canteen cup of barely warm water. After a couple minutes in the water, notionally warmed by the sputtering little fire, we were quickly running out of time.

With about 3min left, it was eat now or go hungry. I looked at the squad leader. He said "ok, we need to do it now." Each Fire Team gets a canteen cup. Bon appetite."

18 guys had a dinner, the sole meal of the day, consisting of 2 tablespoons of warm water, feathers, and a maybe a chicken bone.

The Ranger School Peer Eval
At the end of each phase, every squad had to conduct anonymous Peer Evaluations. In these, you rated your squadmates, starting with 1 for the best guy in the squad, and incrementing for each other squad member. If you had 15 guys in the squad, you'd give the guy you perceived to be least useful a 15. The criteria was kind of fuzzy. It could be a matter of strength and endurance or skills, but most often it was something related to attitude. "Trying your ass off" and "helping your buddies" were attributes held in high regard.

Later that day the guy that got the worst score would be asked by a Ranger Instructor to step over and talk for a minute. You'd never see the guy again. At Darby Phase, the first of the four phases in the woods, 2 guys were taken from our squad.

Losing people via the Peer Evals wasn't a big deal initially. In Darby phase we had some weak Ranger Candidates in the squad, but by the time we'd gotten thru Mountain Phase, those that remained were trying pretty damned hard, and we'd all gotten pretty tight. Sure, there were a few chafing points in the family where a couple guys perceived some minor slight, real or imagined, but for most of us, as we struggled together thru significant adversity, the idea of Peering a squadmate didn't sit well.

By definition, someone had to come in last during Peer Evaluations. However, if the squad was highly motivated and organized, they could defeat the inevitable "someone gets last" consequence of the Peer Eval system by sitting everyone in a rough circle and each person agreeing to anonymously rate everyone in the order that they sat in the circle. That would give everyone in the squad the exact same score, and no one would get Peered Out. Since the Peer Eval is anonymous, everyone is putting themselves in the hands of the next guy. If someone doesn't go with the plan and punks you, or just screws it up, you'll never know who it was that caused a good guy to get Peered Out.

At the end of the Florida (Swamp) Phase, my squad was handed Peer Eval forms. One or two of the guys in the squad that were informal leaders due to their competence and charisma, as opposed to say, me, had broached the idea of rigging the Peer Eval to protect everyone. We had all agreed to do this and therefore not Peer anyone out.

At the end of the phase there was a bit of chaos as folks were moving in different directions trying to get gear ready to leave the field site. Right in the middle of those distractions they sat us down and handed each of us a Peer Eval form. We started to fill it out but then those informal leaders paused us and looked each one of us in the eye. It wasn't something we could talk about because we were being watched. But we understood that we were being told to slow down and focus on our commitment to defeat the Peer Eval.

We moved around a bit, trying to be nonchalant, to form a rough circle. Then we filled out our forms and handed them in.

After about 30min a couple Ranger Instructors grabbed us out of our tasks, had us stand in a formation, and yelled at us a bit. They threatened to recycle the whole bunch of us if we didn't fill out the Peer Eval paperwork honestly. They gave us new Peer Eval forms.

This time we had enough space to whisper. The informal leaders led a quick discussion re. what we were going to do. Everyone was legitimately terrified of being Recycled, but most of the group thought that Recycling the whole lot of us was an empty threat. We agreed to do it again. Frankly, I figured that one or two would not stick with the plan. The forms were anonymous after all. And then the wrong guy would get Peered.

When those forms got tallied up, we really got a ration of shit from the Ranger Instructors. My squadmates had accepted risk and stood up for each other. It was odd to want so badly to smile at your buddies while you're getting your ass chewed. It was a proud day. The Ranger Instructors acted plenty pissed, but being there for your buddy is such a fundamental Ranger idea, that I'm not sure that their heart was in the ass-chewing and threats. Ultimately they let it go. We'd protected each other and no one was Peered out that last day of the FL swamp phase.

Airborne Insertions.
We "jumped" into each phase, so there were 4 jumps. I was pretty damned new to this whole Airborne thing, having done my very first jumps in Airborne School immediately prior to Ranger School.

Jump School had been pretty much a joke. Sure, it was a bit spooky to step out of an airplane 800' up, but if you could just make yourself do that, everything else would probably work out ok. Jump School was 8 hours of honest training compressed into 3wks. The Ranger School jumps, however, were more stressful.

All the Ranger School jumps were at night. All of the jumps were into drop zones seemingly the size of postage stamps. All of the jumps were with full gear, which weighed more than I did. All of the jumps were, it seemed to me the Airborne novice, complete chaos. All of the jumps hurt. All of the jumps resulted in injuries that sent Ranger Candidates home. All of the jumps scared the shit out of me. Ah, I mean caused lots of legitimate concern.

We'd approach a drop zone in a C130 or C141. The big cargo plane would do some sort of nap of the Earth thing in the final approach so the 200lbs of weight suspended by the big buckles on your clavicles would get some g-loading. By the time you finally got to the damned Drop Zone, you were in so much pain because of the buckles digging into your clavicles that you didn't really care if you lived or died. You just wanted out that damned door so you could get the weight off of those buckles.

Most of the weight was in our rucksacks which were suspended from the harness by buckles at our waist. You couldn't really walk with all this weight hanging down in front of your legs, but if you splayed your legs out as far as they would go, you could make an undignified waddle for short distances.

In Jump School there was a carefully choreographed aircraft exit routine of one jumper/sec out the door. In real jumps tho, everyone needs to get out as close to each other as possible so the group doesn't get spread out across the DZ (Drop Zone). That means that the jumpers need to get out the door in a compact mass.

Imagine you and your buddies each have the better part of 200 pounds of gear strapped to your chest, belly, and a leg. You can't really walk like this because your 120 pound rucksack is hanging down from your belly-button to your ankles. So you move around in an inelegant splay-legged waddle. You and your mates are in a tightly packed queue facing a door in the rear of the plane. Everyone is pressing on each other's gear in full body contact. Suddenly someone says go and you all waddle-rush to the door and explode out of it like toothpaste exiting a stomped tube.

It took only a second or two to get to the door. We were each tightly pressed together in the queue, and flew out the door in a spray of humanity. I went out the door lying on top of the guy in front of me, and someone and their gear was lying my back as we tumbled into the windstream.

Because the Drop Zones (DZ) were small, they dropped us pretty low in order to reduce the chance of folks going astray.

Once I got out the door I was tossed ass-over-teakettle by the windstream. Just after I lost physical contact with the guys fore and aft, there'd be a hard yank as the chute filled and my horizontal velocity went from 160mph to 0 in a fraction of a second. I looked up into the darkness an attempt to confirm my was seemed ok, and I exclaimed "Jesus Christ!" in an expression gratitude for being out of the goddamned plane, and also acknowledging the madness of the tumble and chute opening. I then looked down to see what I was falling into and reached down to the pull cords that would allow my ruck and my rifle to come free of my harness and slide down their lanyard and land before me.

If I could pull those release cords, a lot of weight would drop on a long tether. This would mean that there'd be a nice last second deccel once they hit the ground. If I could pull those damned cords in time, I wouldn't hit the ground so damned hard. That never worked.

I couldn't see a goddamned thing. I couldn't see the pull cords nor could I see the ground. Falling through the darkness, utterly helpless, as he invisible ground rushed towards me, all really seemed quite insane. Inevitably, while still fumbling trying to find the pull cords, I slammed into the ground with incredible force.

After rebounding off of the ground like a rag doll, I reached for my chute release rings so I could disconnect the chute from my harness. If I didn't get the chute disconnected, it could catch a wind gust. The ignominy of being dragged around the DZ by your chute was to be avoided at all costs. Dings heal. Humiliation is forever.

Chute released, I laid there for a moment, in whatever awkward position I found myself, a big pile of gear, bruised and winded human, lots parachute cord and silk, as likely lying on my face up-ended in a ditch as anything else, and just try to bring the conscious brain back on line. Then I pulled the release cords on my ruck sack and weapon. The same release cords that I was supposed to have time to pull while I was still in the air.

I then inventoried body parts by moving individual breakable things to see how they fared. My various bent and bruised parts seem to function so I struggled to my hands and knees and paused on all fours to gather myself for a moment.

After a couple seconds of self-pity, I pulled the chute bag out of my ruck and stuffed the chute into it. Then I expertly flipped the 120lb ruck over my head and on to my back, grabbed my rifle and the chute bag, and hustled thru the dark and unfamiliar terrain in the same direction the others seemed to be going. Hopefully they were headed to the chute collection point, because I didn't have the first clue where the hell I was.

I had survived another damned jump. Charlie Mike (Militaryspeak for CM-Continue Mission).

Tim Parks, Ranger Buddy.
The finest thing a human ever did for me was in Ranger. We were in the swamp phase in Florida and we were paddling a rubber raft up a river through a pounding rainstorm. We paddled very hard. Not so much because we were in a big hurry, but because we were freezing our asses off. The ambient temp was warm enough but the rain pouring on us was darn cold. If one paddled at a sustainable intensity, your teeth started chattering. If you stopped paddling for a moment, your body would become so wracked with shivers that you

could hardly control your limbs. Only by paddling good and hard could you generate enough heat to keep the cold at bay.

The swamps of the Florida phase were the low point of Ranger School. By then the lack of sleep, and chow had become critical, and with a couple brief exceptions, we hadn't been dry in 6 weeks. As a result, our skin was rotting off. Our feet were a constant source of problems but with obsessive focus on dry socks we were hanging in there. We always had socks hanging off our rucks in the hopes that we could get a pair to dry. The skin on our knees got abused by us frequently "taking a knee." The skin on our shoulders, waist and crotch was always taking a beating. In places our skin rotted and sloughed off. We stumbling gait, gaunt faces, and skin problems made us look like a zombie movie casting call.

For hours we paddled our way through the swamps. Theoretically we were in a river of sorts, but it didn't look much like a river. It was a meandering passage of less dense vegetation, in an otherwise endless world of dark and forbidding trees. The trees seemed perched on root systems that started several feet above the water, than disappeared down below until your shin found them.

After an eternity, the squad leader of the day pointed to the "shore," which looked to me was a mass of tree roots indistinguishable from all the other masses of tree roots we'd passed. We could have been miles from where we were supposed to be for all I knew. I certainly couldn't have estimated how far we'd navigated up the "river. By "shore", I mean the water was 2' deep, not 6'.

I was too exhausted to care. If it turned out that we were in the wrong place, it wasn't my problem. I'd go thru the motions and do everything I could help the poor bastards in leadership positions that day to succeed, but it wasn't my mission. If it turned out to be a cock-up, it wasn't my cock-up. I was nearing the end of what I had to give. It was everything I could do to just keep driving on one minute to the next.

We had been kneeling in the rubber boat for hours, sitting on our legs as we paddled hard. As a result of the extended time in the awkward sitting position, now that we'd arrived, we couldn't seem to operate our legs. We ended up just rolling out of the boat and crawling pitifully to "shore," dragging our rucks behind. It was a difficult moment. I was pretty messed up. I was almost in tears with desperation to find more reserves. I was starving to death, I'd not seen an hour's uninterrupted sleep in weeks, I was freezing cold, thoroughly exhausted, and I was reduced to crawling like an infant dragging my 120lb rucksack over the submerged roots because my legs, screaming with pain, wouldn't work.

I was in trouble. After an eight year struggle to both pay for and complete the mechanical engineering degree, I'd decided instead to "see what I was made of". I was determined to prove that I had more tenacity and fitness, that I was more capable, than most anyone else around. I had decided to become and Army Infantry Officer as the first step towards being a leader in Special Forces. First it would be the Rangers, then Special Forces, than I would attempt to try out for Delta.

However, I was in trouble. The weeks of exhaustion, sleep and chow deprivation, and exposure, had sucked the life out of me. I was at the end of my rope. I was shivering uncontrollably in two feet of water. My cramped leg muscles felt like they had daggers in them. I couldn't seem to make them work. I was in a fetal position using my ruck to keep my chest out of the water. I just had nothing left to give.

That's when my "Ranger Buddy," Tim Parks, unwrapped a field ration cookie bar, took a bite and said "here" giving me the other half. That was the single finest thing anyone has ever done for me. As long as I live I will never forget the rush of gratitude I felt when Parks gave me half of that MRE cookie bar, as I laid there shivering, exhausted, and half submerged in cold dark water. While the leadership spent 10min in a huddle trying to figure something out, I savored the cookie bar by eating it slowly in little rat-like nibbles. Somehow that gesture, and that cookie bar, opened up new reserves. I wasn't dead yet. I could keep moving.

Later that night we were trudging along through knee deep water. Parks and I were leading the patrol. We weren't in charge, I think he had been directed to be "compass man" and I'd been directed to be "pace count" which meant it was up to me to keep track of how many steps we took so we'd know how far we've moved.

Everyone had strengths and weaknesses. Each person in a leadership position for the day had to pick his key people very carefully. His success or failure could easily hinge on a good/bad choice.

On a patrol, I was pretty dependable at pace count, staying awake, and as a pack mule. No matter what kind of chaos occurred during the patrol, I wouldn't lose track of the pace count."

Carrying 120lbs of rucksack, weapon, and water, Parks and I trudged for hours at the front of the platoon. It was pretty dark with little starlight filtering thru the canopy up above, but it was clear that we'd been moving up a gradual slope for much of this time.

I marveled at how the water stayed about knee deep the whole time, just deep enough to conceal roots to bang our shins against. I tried to understand how we could walk up a gentle slope yet the water remained at the same level. Coming out of college as an engineer, I'd had a lot of physics. For the water to remain level on this slope would require a gravity vector that was a tad off-center. That seemed pretty darn unlikely but it was hard to deny the evidence before me. Clearly the water was lying flat on this gradual uphill slope. So even tho I didn't understand the why of it, something was clearly going on with gravity. I vaguely recalled something I'd read years prior about certain places on the Earth's surface where gravity works in odd ways. I hadn't paid much attention to the article at the time but it certainly seemed to explain what I was experiencing.

Of course there was no uphill slope. I was starting to hallucinate.

That's when Parks whispered to me that he'd noted a light up ahead, conveniently on our compass bearing so that was going to be his reference point.

I didn't see any light.

We kept going like this for a couple hours, banging shins into or tripping over submerged roots constantly. Multiple times Parks reiterated that we were heading for "that light up there" and I'd peer intently ahead into the dark forest of trees perched on their supporting tree roots. But I saw no light in the distance. Finally I stopped Parks and we had a whispered conversation.

"Dude, there…is….no….light up there. No light."

Parks: "Sure there is. We've been moving towards it all night."

"I'm telling you man, there's no light. We're really fucking tired and we're seeing things. There's no light."

Parks: "Look. Right there. A light."

<The Plt Ldr and Sqd Ldr sloged up> The Plt Ldr whispered, "What's the problem?"

"Parks says he sees a light up there that we've been heading towards for hours. I don't see this light. Who's "Alternate Compass?" <I asked this because there's supposed to be another guy in the platoon that has been watching the azimuth that we've been traveling on. He could tell us if we'd drifted off

course>

<We all looked at each other. No one could remember who the hell was Alternate Compass guy. When you're that tired, if you don't write it down, it doesn't get remembered. While we were whispering, the rest of the platoon had moved up and automatically faced outboard, forming a hasty perimeter. The Plt Ldr whispered to the group:
"Who is Alternate Compass?" <No response>
"Who the fuck is Alternate Compass?" <Still no response>
<Turning back to us> "Well. Fuck."

It did all work out. Even tho Parks led us on a chase for an imaginary light half the night, he did it in pretty much a straight line. The OPFOR that night obligingly lit a fire. The Ranger Instructors might have gotten a little anxious that we'd lost our way in the miles of almost impenetrable swamp. So once we spotted the glow of the fire, we were able to complete the mission.

The crushing failure. Recycling in the desert.
It was a bitter brutal blow. It was so unfair that I will grind my teeth over it to the end of my days. I was a leadership failure in the Utah desert. As a result I did not graduate with Ranger Class 12-89, but instead languished in misery, albeit sleep and chow filled misery, for a month until the next Ranger Class (13-89) came to town.

In each phase, each of us were evaluated in a leadership position. In one of the last missions of Ranger School, I was designated the Weapons Squad Leader for a platoon mission. At this point we'd been doing all this for so long, we could practically do it in our sleep. The required leadership tasks that had at first seemed at first to be a list way impossibly long to remember and execute properly, now seemed like second nature. Any one of us could take over any planning or leadership role in the platoon and done just fine w/o really having to try that hard. We all knew the various jobs forwards and backwards. What's more, when every single person knows the tasks that you need to accomplish, a lot gets done for you pretty much on autopilot.

After two months of this, we were professional Ranger Candidates. We had the routine down pat.

The operation was a live-fire raid. We were going to hit an objective, sweep through fast, and then withdraw. As Weapons Sqd Leader, I was in charge of three or four M60 machine gun teams. Our role was to provide covering fire from some high ground 4-500yrds behind the friendlies and a little bit to one side. We'd fire into the objective only a few dozen yards in front of our buddies. Then as the squads assaulted the objective we'd shift fire to the center of the objective, then ultimately to the far side. When the squads pulled back to their assault locations, we'd resume our fires on to the objective to suppress the enemy so they didn't get any ideas about firing upon our withdrawing squads. We'd be putting rounds pretty darn close to our friends. We'd have to be very careful.

We'd all been working together a long time. We'd done missions like this several times. This was no big deal.

I had a problem though. M60 machine guns have weak firing pins. They tend to break. As a result, a genuine M60 machine gunner always carried an extra firing pin. When we got the M60 machine guns a couple weeks prior, only two of them came with working firing pins. Someone must have figured, "it's only training, it's not a big deal."

Another firing pin broke the previous evening and the Ranger Instructors did not seem inclined to get us more firing pins. That left us with three or four machine guns for training purposes, but only one that would fire.

We had extra barrels so we could change them if the rate of fire was high enough that the barrels got too hot, we just had no extra firing pins.

So I was in a pickle. I figured that in some ways I had to go thru the motions and act as if we really did have three or four machine guns, but in other ways I had to accept the reality that only one of them actually worked.

So when the weapons squad moved up to the support-by-fire position, each machine gun team had ammo and their extra barrel. But once they started shooting, I moved all ammo, and all extra barrels to the one M60 that could really shoot. They blew thru an assload of rounds, had great fun shooting right in front of their buddies, changed barrels as the squads assaulted thru the objective, and fired like crazy to cover the withdrawing squads. It was really great fun.

When it was time for my Weapons Squad to withdraw, I redistributed the spare barrels, but I left the remaining ammunition with the one M60 that could go fire.

Later, in my evaluation the Ranger Instructor criticized me for failing to redistribute the ammunition. I told him that it wasn't a failure, it was the plan. I left the ammunition with the M60 that had the good firing pin.

To which he responded that I'd failed the critical squad leader task of redistribution of ammunition.

My "but, but, but, but, that was the plan. Only the one gun worked" didn't seem to impress him. This meant that I'd failed a leadership position. That was a Recycle. My eyes went wide and I was motionless with horror. I never understood why he didn't understand that I'd intentionally left the ammo with that M60. Maybe he thought I'd made that up to cover my failure, I don't know.

The next day was the last mission. I was screwed. At the end of the mission there were quiet celebrations because it was finally over. We'd made it. Except for me. I was a Recycle.

All my friends that I'd gone thru hell with these past months were besides themselves with joy that they'd made it. They were sorry for me, sure. It was clear that I'd gotten a raw deal, but they were so damned relieved and happy that they'd finally made it to the end of Ranger, that it was hard for them to re-orient on my horror.

The 4wks of being a recycle were a strange time. I was furious at being punked, but also resigned to the fact that there was no damned use in being angry about it. I needed to shrug it off and drive on. There was a tremendous sense of failure. I started thinking, for the first time, of contingency plans for a scenario where I did not earn the Ranger Tab.

I had chosen to walk away from my engineering degree and become an Infantry Officer as a stepping stone to the various elite Special Operations Forces. I wanted to be a Ranger, and then be a Green Beret. Then I wanted to try out for Delta. I wanted to see what I was made of.

But all that was going to fall like a house of cards if I failed to get the Ranger Tab. So if that happened, I decided to call this Army thing temporary insanity and I would take whatever crappy Army job I was assigned to after washing out of Ranger School and then I would get out as soon as I could.

Mostly tho, I ate and slept. And felt sorry for myself.

To my delight, I had a friend among the recycles. Well, he was none too pleased to be among the 8 or so of us, but for me it was darn nice to be able to hang out and commiserate with Bidwell, an acquaintance from both Infantry Officer Basic and Officer Candidate School.

Bidwell was a really nice guy. Not a real gung ho charismatic guy, but he was smart, tenacious, reliable, and the fact that he'd made it all the way to the Desert phase would seem to indicate that he had unexpected toughness. We'd not been in the same platoon in Infantry Officer Basic nor OCS, so we didn't really know each other well. But we got pretty tight during our recycle month. Bidwell and already recycled once. He'd started in Ranger Class 11-89 while I went off to Airborne School. Then he'd recycled into my Class 12-89, gotten Peered Out and would be going into 13-89 with me.

As a recycle, I mostly I ate and slept. There were a few make-work tasks for us, but no one had their heart into bothering us much. For the first couple weeks, at each meal, I'd eat myself until I was absolutely stuffed.....So completely full that I felt that I might throw up. Then I'd go back to my room, pull out my bowl of candy bars, and see if I couldn't fit a bit more in my belly. I couldn't stop myself. Day after day was like that. I'd eat until I thought I was going to die. Then I'd lean against something until the wave of nausea abated. Then I'd reach for another candy bar.

Un-Recycled. Joining our new platoon in the desert.
When we linked up with our new platoon, it was initially pretty awkward. They were a bunch of strangers, skeletal strangers straight from that absolute horror that broke so many of us, Florida's Swamp Phase. We were looking at them before they had any chance to recover from their mental and physical nadir. They were also a family. They'd gone thru hell together, they'd supported each other thru the bleakest of times, therefore they were tight-knit.

Bidwell, and I, on the other hand, were outsiders. Failures. Pudgy cheeked fat failures, that had shared no privations at their side, and had no track record of reliability under stress. We might be ok guys, but Bidwell and I were not family. And when it came time for Peer Evals, family protected family. Bidwell and I were in trouble.

If Bidwell and I were going to make it, we had to be so fabulous, generate so much gratitude with our efforts to help others, that members of this family would decide to Peer Out family members in order to protect these new fat guys. This was not going to be easy.

In Utah's high desert, the nights started turning cold in Sept. Unlike the earlier phases, we were getting more time in laager sites and often got honest couple hours of sleep. This was a safety precaution because of all the live fire exercises during the Desert Phase.

After hitting an objective we would rapidly move away to the pre-planned rally point. From there we'd move to a laager site many miles away. In the desert, we'd choose a bowl shaped depression, set up security and observation around the high ground, then get some sleep in shifts curled up inside of the depression formed by sand berms on the hard desert floor. We didn't have coats or blankets. We had only our uniform shirts, properly called "blouses" and the threadbare t-shirts underneath.

During the day the temperature would be a comfortable low humidity 80's. Then the temperature would plummet down to freezing at night. We had to cuddle up in order to make it thru the night. If you were in a fighting or observation position, you would cuddle up tight with your Ranger Buddy. If you were in a sleep shift, you'd get into the mob of everyone else. The mob of folks trying to stay warm while they slept was never stationary. People had to get up and do their time on the perimeter and vice versa. If you, while fast asleep, weren't actively worming yourself into the center, then you were being pushed out towards the edge. You didn't want to be on the outer edge because it was damned cold there.

When I was awoken my uniform was covered in frost. I was so cold that I couldn't move. Desperate to generate some heat, I'd strain start crawling around a little to get my arms and legs moving. Once I could move a bit more, I'd do some pushups and situps to recover from the couple hours spent as a human corpsicle.

With no jacket not stocking cap, go take a two hour nap in a meat locker and you'll see what it's like.

My Recycle buddy Ranger Bidwell had already been Peered Out in the Desert. I'd never been Peered. I don't recall the exact dynamic of it, but somehow the situation was that if Bidwell got Peered again he would wash out of Ranger School.

Bidwell was burned out. He really hadn't been kicking ass and taking names like a retread needed to do to survive. Instead, he complained. I had some hard conversations with him over the two weeks, our second tour of Utah's Desert Phase. I was worried that he was going to get Peered again so I pressed on him hard to get his damned act together. I think though, that he was just too burned out to care. The other Ranger Candidates were complaining to me about Mark. The situation was bad.

The day before Peer Evals I dreamed up a solution. I would get the squad to Peer me out instead of Bidwell. Since I'd never been Peered out, I could survive getting Peered in this last phase, so only my pride would be hurt. Bidwell couldn't survive another Peer Out and that seemed to be the way the wind was blowing.

Over the course of the day I talked to each squad member about Bidwell. I told them that he was a really good dude, but having recycled twice, he'd done far more of this then the rest of us. He was just exhausted. I asked them that if they decided the next day to Peer Out Bidwell, to write my name instead.

The next day we got our Peer Eval sheets. Of course they were handed to us when we were busy with other distractions. It's hard to remember things when you're tired and distracted, but I got the attention of each person in the squad individually and gave them "the look" to remind them. It worked. I got Peered, but it didn't matter. Bidwell and I both graduated in September, 1989. Jesus Christ what a summer.

Weeks later Bidwell would end up in a neighboring Brigade

near us in Korea. We spent an evening together at the bars in the nearby Korean ville every month or so. He was a great guy.

The end.

Scott Gress, Savannah, GA. MAJ, US Army (Retired)